Praise for *Is It My Fault?*

"This book is a tour de force of wisdom, goodness, and compassion for those who know the agony and shame of domestic violence and for every leader who interacts with more than four families in a year. One out of every four homes in America will experience domestic abuse and it is no different in the church than in the so-called secular world. In fact, conservative Christians are more likely to remain in violence and think it is biblical. This treasure of a book invites the reader into a sweeping and life giving understanding of the Bible's view of women, violence, suffering, and redemption that if embraced would radically alter how victims and care givers address this heartache. This is a must-read book."

DAN B. ALLENDER
Professor of Counseling Psychology and founding president of the Seattle School of Theology and Psychology

"The authors' deeply compassionate writing offers us a book that does not merely speak to us, it comes along beside us—offering both experience and in-depth knowledge about this emotionally charged subject. Too often the church has been not merely been silent but complicit in protecting abusers and marginalizing victims. Justin and Lindsey's book takes us in a new direction of hope, healing, and mercy. I am more than happy to commend this book."

GREGORY O. BREWER
Bishop of the Episcopal Diocese of Central Florida

"Domestic abuse is an area where sincere but uninformed 'help' can hurt. Unfortunately, even the misuse of Scripture, often by well-meaning Christians, can become part of the problem. Justin and Lindsey serve the church well by defining what abuse is, what Scripture says, how victims should respond, and how pastor-counselors can be effectively involved. This is a must-read for pastors, victims, and friends of victims. This issue is too prevalent and devastating to be ignored. The blind eye of the church hurts those without a voice. Read this book and become equipped to effectively care for those whose cry is reaching the e   waiting for a hand from the body of Christ."

BRAD HAMBRICK
*Pastor of counseling at   nd
author of Self-Cente   en
Marriages*

"This is it. This is the book on domestic violence that needs to be sitting on every pastor's desk, required reading for every seminarian, and the next book discussed among church leadership, in book clubs, Bible studies, home groups, and lay counselor trainings. Not only do Justin and Lindsey compassionately and responsibly define domestic violence, identify its signs, its cycles, and its effects on the victims and their communities, they take us to Scripture to reveal God's heart for those unnecessarily afflicted and trapped in violent domestic relationships. Each person who reads this book will have a better understanding of how to identify domestic violence in their own relationships or in those of people they know, love, and minister to. And with a thorough appendix of practical information and steps to take, both the victims and the ones supporting them will gain the insight and clarity they need to prevent the violence from happening again."

MONICA TAFFINDER
Cofounder and counselor, Grace Clinic Christian Counseling

"While reading this book I found myself regularly exclaiming 'Amen!' and 'Come on!' to Lindsey and Justin's wisdom and biblical understanding of the issues. This book is a valuable and important resource for Christian women who have experienced abuse and for all those who want to support them. Lindsey and Justin invite the Christian community to honor and value women and children and to no longer collude with, perpetuate, or indeed perpetrate abuse against those whom God has created. I have been looking for a book to recommend to women in the conservative Christian church and their supporters; this book is ideal."

NATALIE COLLINS
Activist working to end violence against women and gender injustice; founder of the DAY Programme and Spark

"In simple, eloquent prose, Justin and Lindsey Holcomb shine a light on the darkness surrounding domestic violence. As detailed in the accounts of survivors, the very husbands and fathers charged with the care of their families sometimes represent the greatest threat. Equally troublesome, many clergy and church leaders routinely support offenders and ostracize victims. In making clear that God stands with the suffering, this book offers survivors a path to healing and the church a path to reform."

VICTOR VIETH
Executive Director, National Child Protection Training Center; child protection attorney; author

"Justin and Lindsey have done it again! Their book on sexual abuse, *Rid My Disgrace*, and now this one, *Is It My Fault?*, are gifts to the church, its leaders, and especially to those who suffer from the horror and pain of sexual assault and domestic violence. In this book you will find compassionate, practical, biblical, and grace-based help for those who suffer and for those who love and want to help those who suffer. If you are a pastor or a leader and care, this is not an optional book. You will 'rise up and call' Justin and Lindsey blessed for writing it . . . and, more important, those to whom you minister will, too."

STEVE BROWN
Host, Key Life Radio Program; author, Three Free Sins: God Isn't Mad At You

"Domestic violence demands silence—perpetrators don't want to be exposed, and victims are too ashamed to speak. Justin and Lindsey counter that silence with words and deeds. They give words to describe it, words to speak to the Lord, words that remind us of the truth, such as 'It is never my fault' and 'He [God] delights in us,' and deeds that can bring the violence to an end."

ED WELCH
Counselor and Faculty, the Christian Counseling and Educational Foundation; author

"The roots of domestic violence and the resulting wounds and scars are deep and enduring. So I am very grateful for the wisdom and expertise of Justin and Lindsey Holcomb in helping the church understand and apply the biblical requirements of justice and accountability and the biblical promises of healing and hope. The Holcombs' work is a gift from God to all of us and a valuable ministry of Christ's restorative gospel for those who have suffered great harm."

JARED WILSON
Pastor of Middletown Springs Community Church and author of Gospel Wakefulness

"One of every four women you know has or will face intimate partner violence. What does the God of Scripture say to them? In this rich and rare resource, Justin and Lindsey Holcomb combine their theological and practical training to offer these women a way out of both abuse and the shame and despair that accompany it. They show powerfully how the 'one-way violence' of abusers is overcome by the 'one-way love' of God in Christ. I recommend this book to every church leader looking for a truly Christ-centered response to domestic violence in their midst."

KATELYN BEATY
Managing Editor, Christianity Today

"Could the gospel be not just for sinners, but for victims? Having worked with many who have been impacted by psychological, sexual, and physical abuse, I am so grateful for this book. It reminds me, once again, that the gospel is indeed good news—particularly to those who have been victimized."

CHUCK DEGROAT
Associate Professor of Pastoral Care and Counseling, Western Theological Seminary; senior fellow, Newbigin House of Studies; and author of Toughest People to Love

"The Holcombs offer an 'intervention of grace' to those who suffer under domestic violence. They show that the God of the Bible abounds in grace and love, restoring dignity and hope to those who've been harmed. Victims will find a voice to speak out about the violence they've endured, guided by the very words of Scripture, and they will find a God who acts with righteous power to rescue the oppressed."

MIKE WILKERSON
Author, Redemption: Freed by Jesus from the Idols We Worship and the Wounds We Carry

"Specific, tender, concrete, compassionate, bold, understanding, wise, and dyed with the gorgeous gospel of grace that is ours in Christ Jesus. I love this book! It unpacks the experience of the victim without ever feeling coldly analytical. It gives you important things to consider and clear steps to take without ever pushing you. Read it and you'll feel loved, understood, and helped, but best of all you'll rest in the love of Jesus more than you have before."

PAUL TRIPP
President of Paul Tripp Ministries; executive director of the Center for Pastoral Life and Care in Fort Worth, Texas; and author of A Shelter in the Time of Storm: Meditations on God and Trouble

IS IT MY FAULT?

HOPE AND HEALING FOR THOSE SUFFERING DOMESTIC VIOLENCE

JUSTIN S. HOLCOMB | LINDSEY A. HOLCOMB

MOODY PUBLISHERS

CHICAGO

Edited by Stephanie S. Smith of (In)dialogue Communications
Interior design: Ragont Design
Cover Design: Faceout Studio
Cover Image: Shutterstock #4828659
Author photo: Kim Bogardus

ISBN: 978-0-8024-1024-5

We hope you enjoy this book from Moody Publishers. Our goal is to provide high-quality, thought-provoking books and products that connect truth to your real needs and challenges. For more information on other books and products written and produced from a biblical perspective, go to www.moodypublishers.com or write to:

Moody Publishers
820 N. LaSalle Boulevard
Chicago, IL 60610

1 3 5 7 9 10 8 6 4 2

Printed in the United States of America

Contents

Foreword

Is it my fault?" Perhaps you have picked this book up because that's a question you've asked yourself; perhaps it's a question that you are not sure you know the answer to or because there is someone in your life whom you once trusted who tells you that the abuse you're facing is your fault. Perhaps you're even afraid to pick the book up at all . . . and you're wondering right now where you could hide it so that person won't see it. Pick it up anyway.

If you are still able to hope that there may be a way out of the nightmare you're living, then this book is for you.

The first thing you'll learn here is that you are not alone. You are not alone because what you are faced with on a daily basis is the common experience of millions of other women, children, and men around the world. You'll learn about that in this book. You'll also learn that you are not alone because, although you may have been told differently, God stands with you and against your abuser. The Lord Jesus knows exactly what abuse is like and He hates it. Yes, He willingly suffered under it, but His suffering was redemptive and had a particular goal. His suffering was different from yours. He loves His bride and wars against all those who would harm her. He loves her. So pick this book up and hide it wherever you need to . . . and learn to rest in His love for you because it will be that as you learn of His love and rest in it you will eventually have the strength to stand against the abuse that you've come to think is normal. It isn't normal. It is sin. You can stand with your Lord against it. The Holcombs will help you understand and believe in that truth.

But this book isn't only for women who are being abused. It is for those who seek to help them. I would feel more comfortable coming to you saying, "This is a great book for helping unbelievers who struggle with violence in their homes, so you should have it on your bookshelf just in case one of those kinds of people happens to wander into your church." If only it were true that the church, a culture that Jesus said was to be known by the love we have for one another, wasn't in great need of a book like this. If only.

Of course the heartbreaking truth is that violence within the Christian community is as prevalent as it is without . . . and possibly worse because Christian women notoriously under-report. Countless women, women who have been loved, made righteous, forgiven and welcomed by Christ, are trapped in hate-filled marriages where their souls are systematically bludgeoned with Satan's lies about their worthlessness and where their bodies are systematically battered by the hands and arms of someone who has promised to love and protect them. This is a great evil and their Husband, the Lord of Heaven and Earth, is storing up deep wrath for those who would treat his Bride in this way, and for a church who would turn her back on these, the weakest among us.

This terrible evil has been exacerbated by a false and injurious overemphasis on gender roles, in particular, the roles of wives who are called to "submit" to their husbands (even in sin) and to try to win them with their "gentle and quiet spirit". . . as if that meant they are to submit themselves to being sinned against without breathing a word of it to anyone. Quietness about domestic violence is not the message that Peter was communicating in this passage. His message was rather a message of hope, that the wife of a disobedient man had other means at her disposal to win him . . . that she didn't need to rely on her words alone. The truth is that the most loving action an abused woman can take is to seek, in whatever way possible, to bring conviction of sin to her husband, that he might repent and not face the wrath of her Heavenly Husband who will certainly bring His hand of discipline down to protect her.

This false and damning teaching has consigned thousands of our Christian sisters and their children to life in a virtual solitary confinement, to a life that frequently ends in a violent death. The truth is that every nine seconds a woman in the United States is assaulted or beaten. "It is the leading cause of injury to women—more than car accidents, muggings and rapes combined."[1] Homicide is among the leading causes of death for women in the African-American community. "Around the world at least one in every three women has been beaten, coerced into sex, or otherwise abused during her lifetime. Most often, the abuser is a member of her own family."[2] And in most cases women are unable or unwilling to report because they are ashamed, afraid, or misinformed. Some Christian women have been wrongly taught that their primary goal in life is to protect their husband's reputation and standing in the church so that he is "praised in the gates." This great blight on the name of Christ and our churches is further perpetrated by an enemy who has hated women and sought to damage them from the very beginning of time.

This terrible evil isn't confined only to ghettos or among those who are ignorant or unchurched. In fact, while I was reading the Holcombs' wonderful manuscript, I had to ask if I could send it on to a pastor friend who was counseling a good friend of mine who is in a deeply abusive marriage and who needed his help getting free. The truth is that we all need the wise and biblical training presented here so that the noxious misogynistic miasma that has infiltrated our churches in the name of gender roles and "submission" can be replaced by the fresh air of the gospel: a gospel that honors the dignity and value of women and children and that stands in the gap to protect those who are the "least of these" among us.

Read this book. Give it to your pastors and staff and encourage them to send a strong message to the men and women in their congregation: Abuse and violence needs to be reported and will be taken seriously by the church. Women will not be blamed, shamed, ostracized, or excommunicated for reporting; they will be protected.

It is my hope that this book, written by a husband and wife who have taken up the God-given mantle of protecting women and children, will give you the courage and the boldness to protect the women and children among you ... and if you dare, to step into the gap and call abusers and batterers to repent—for the sake of their own souls.

ELYSE M. FITZPATRICK, counselor, author, speaker

Introduction

If you are reading this, it's likely that you know more about domestic violence than you ever wanted to—simply because you've lived it.

Your experience is and has been very painful, fearful, confusing, and traumatizing. Maybe you don't even know entirely its effects on your life, or what exactly to make of it all.

You may be in the midst of violence and abuse as you read this— and you're desperate for a way out. The sense of feeling trapped can be paralyzing and overwhelming. If you feel you are in danger, please call 911 or go to appendix 1: "Getting Help" for practical steps to make sure you remain safe—and that your children, if you have children, also remain safe.

Perhaps the violence you experienced happened last week or decades ago, and thankfully, you are now safe. However, the effects of domestic abuse can last long after one is physically safe, as you are likely figuring out.

Or maybe you are reading this and you know something isn't quite right, but you are not sure what to call it. Maybe you think "abuse" seems too harsh a word for your experience, so you construct explanations for why this person hurts you, or you blame yourself, or you are hoping and praying he or she will change in time.

You are not alone. The number of occurrences of domestic violence is staggering. At least one in four women become victims of domestic violence in her lifetime.[1]

We wrote this book for the many victims of domestic violence, who are predominately women, to offer accessible, gospel-based help, hope, and healing. In other words, we wrote this book for you.

Our hope is that this book will encourage you to believe that God knows and sees your suffering, and that God cares about you and hears your cries and prayers. He cares for you so much that He wants you safe and delivered from threat and violence. If you have children, He wants them safe too. But even beyond physical safety, God wants you to heal from the many ways you've been hurt and wounded. We pray that this book is one of the tools God uses for your own protection and healing process.

But because the healing process is best aided in the context of community, this book is also for the family, friends, clergy, and ministry staff who want to love and support victims of abuse.

Many people want to help those in their family or circle of friends who are being hurt by domestic violence, but they don't always know how. They are often overwhelmed by the seriousness of the situation and feel helpless to lend adequate support. But here, they couldn't be more wrong. Friends, family, and ministry members can offer *immense* help and support to victims of abuse.

The alternate effect of this, of course, is that some "help"—if mis-applied—can actually hurt. Platitudes, prying questions, and shallow "biblical" answers, for example, do more harm than good for a victim who feels stuck in a desperate situation. In fact, many victims believe clergy have the most potential to help them, when in reality they are too often the least helpful and sometimes even harmful.[2]

For this reason, we have combined our theological training with easy-to-understand, step-by-step advice. Both of us have seen the damage that domestic violence wreaks in our culture every day.

Lindsey earned a masters in public health with a focus on vio-lence against women and public health responses, which informs her counseling of domestic violence victims today. She has worked as a case manager at a domestic violence shelter and a sexual assault crisis center. Lindsey has also trained other counselors and volunteers in crisis intervention.

Justin is a minister and has counseled numerous victims of domestic violence. Since 2000, he has taught theology at Reformed Theological Seminary and also teaches at Gordon-Conwell Theological Seminary.

Justin has taught courses on violence against women in the Sociology and Religious Studies departments, as well as in the Studies of Women and Gender program, at the University of Virginia.

We believe that the deepest message of the ministry of Jesus and the Bible is the grace of God to all of us because we are all broken people in a broken world. Grace is most needed and best understood in the midst of sin, suffering, and brokenness.[3] We wrote *Rid of My Disgrace: Hope and Healing for Victims of Sexual Assault* to apply the good news of the grace of God to those suffering from the sense of disgrace due to sexual assault. In *Is It My Fault?* we address the effects of domestic violence with the biblical message of God's grace.

Wherever you are in your experience with abuse—past or present—please understand this: Jesus responds to your pain. Your story does not end with abuse and violence. Your life was intended for more than shame, guilt, fear, anger, and confusion. The abuse does not define you or have the last word on your identity. Yes, it is part of your story, but not the end of your story.

In Jesus, the God who delivers us from evil also offers us a path to healing. And it's time to let this truth transform the shape of your story.

Part 1

WHAT IS
DOMESTIC VIOLENCE?

1

Deliver Us from Evil

Domestic abuse looks different in different households. Sometimes the abuse is physical, and hitting, shouting, or hair-pulling are a regular part of your home. Other times, the abuser won't ever lay a hand on you—but you will be shamed, called names, and manipulated. Maybe you think you did something to spur him on, or that you were too passive or too demanding, or that you are somehow, in some way, to blame for the abuse you are experiencing.

Your experience of domestic abuse may be very different than someone else's, but no matter what, one truth stands the same for all: *It is never your fault.*

No matter what kind of abuse you have experienced, there is nothing you can do, nothing you can say, nothing you think that makes you deserving of it. There is no mistake you could have made and no sin you could have committed to make you deserving of violence.

You do not deserve this. And it is never your fault.

You did not ask for this. You should not be silenced. You are not worthless. You do not have to pretend like nothing happened. You are not damaged goods, forgotten or ignored by God, or "getting what you deserve."

But you are created in the image of God. You should be treated with dignity, love, and respect, but instead you are or were the victim of abuse and violence, and *it was wrong*. You were sinned against.

If you're still not convinced, listen to the opinion of domestic violence expert Lundy Bancroft: "Abuse is not caused by relationship dynamics. You can't manage your partner's abusiveness by changing your behavior, but he wants you to think that you can."[1] Situations of domestic violence are often extremely difficult to deal with, because abusers are often masters of control and manipulation.

If you are in a situation of domestic abuse or think you might be, there's a few things you need to know. First, the abuse is not your fault. Second, while you may feel drained, depressed, frightened, ashamed, and confused, you are not alone. And third, help is available to you.

Maybe the abuse isn't physical—that doesn't mean it's not abuse. Most abuse cases begin with emotional, verbal, and other nonphysical forms of abuse and then escalate to physical forms. Or maybe the abuse has been going on for a while and shows no sign of becoming physical.

It might seem as though "violence" is too intense of a word to describe the kind of abuse that's "only" emotional. Here's what theologian Hans Boersma has to say about that: "Violence need not necessarily be physical. Emotional abuse can be just as damaging as physical abuse—and at times even more so."[2] Ethicist Wolfgang Huber argues that violence is better defined as the intent to hurt or torture, more than physical injury.[3]

The fact that your abuse doesn't send you to the hospital or leave scars doesn't make it any less painful, and it doesn't make it any less wrong. The scars of emotional abuse are very real, they can run very deep, and they are not to be dismissed. In fact, emotional abuse can be just as damaging as physical abuse—sometimes even more so (we'll talk about this more in chapter 4).

Violence seems like an intense word. But that is exactly what the experience of domestic violence is. There is both physical and nonphysical violence. Augustinian Friar Donald X. Burt defines a violent act as "any act which *contravenes the rights* of another. It can also be described as an act which *causes injury* to the life, property, or person of a human being, oneself, or others."[4] Leo. D. Lefebure, a professor at Georgetown University, offers a helpful definition of violence as "the attempt of an individual or group to impose its will on others through any nonverbal, verbal, or physical means that inflict psychological or physical injury."[5]

Naming domestic violence for what it is—and dealing with it as such—is important for this essential reason: the abuse usually gets worse. Infrequent episodes usually progress to more frequent ones. Less severe episodes usually progress to more severe ones. Domestic abuse often escalates from threats and verbal abuse to physical violence. And while physical injury may be the most obvious danger, the emotional and psychological consequences of domestic abuse are also severe.

If you're reading this and see signs that you are in an abusive relationship, we applaud you for having the courage to name what you are experiencing, to call it what it is, and to begin seeking a better way. Because the truth is, you were made for more than this. God loves you and it grieves Him to see you suffer this abuse—whatever it might look like. We applaud you for picking up this book in the first place, which is nothing less than an act of courage.

And we sincerely hope and pray you will next act on that courage by removing yourself from the abuse. This isn't about mustering up more courage to stay with him and continue to put yourself in harm's way. No, this is about courage to do what's best for you by fleeing the abuse altogether, in order to find a physically, emotionally, and spiritually safe place. This is our greatest hope for you.

Of course the process of getting to that safe place will be complicated and multilayered. Because as long as you are in a relationship with an abusive person, the abuse will not simply go away on its own. You don't need to confront him alone, because what you most need is to be safe and we will provide several strategies for this. We will be also very straightforward with you about the sort of dangers you will risk when you break off an abusive relationship so that you know what you will have to watch out for (or, if you are a friend or loved one, what you can help guard against).

The process of getting to that safe place may sound frightening or even impossible at this point, but to stay poses an even greater risk to you and your children, if you have them.

The pain is real, but the healing and hope is just as real. We are convinced, because the Bible teaches it and experience confirms it, that "God is the God of Life, the one who redeems. Our faith teaches us that out of suffering, loss, and death, God brings life."[6] God protects and delivers His people from suffering, abuse, and violence.

Jesus would not have taught us to ask God to "Deliver us from evil," if it were not possible.

DELIVER US FROM EVIL

This truth comes from the Lord's Prayer, which is one of the most well-known passages in the Bible. Here is a traditional version found in Matthew 6:9–13:

> Our Father in heaven,
>   hallowed be your name,
>   your kingdom come,
>   your will be done,
>   on earth as it is in heaven.
> Give us today our daily bread.
> And forgive us our debts,
>   as we also have forgiven our debtors.
> And lead us not into temptation,
>   but deliver us from the evil one.

We're going to spend a minute on this prayer because it is familiar to a lot of Christians and explains why we believe God offers hope—concrete hope—for victims of domestic violence (more on this in chapter 9).

Some of the prayer seems, well, just spiritual. When we pray for God to be honored, to forgive our sins, or to deliver us from temptation, it can seem like we are asking for things to happen on some special spiritual plane apart from the real world. After all, how can we tangibly tell if God is honored?

But then the other half of the prayer asks for concrete, visible things. God's will on earth. Daily bread. And finally—and for us, most importantly—deliverance from evil. These are reminders that God's power extends to the everyday realm and that He is active in our lives.

Not all of the people we meet are trustworthy. Not all of the environments we live in are trustworthy. The ordinary, everyday world is filled with evil and fraught with temptation. This portion of the Lord's Prayer, then, is about asking God to bolster our faith, to give us strength, and to save us from evil and its effects—violence, affliction, and suffering.

This, by the way, is a prayer our heavenly Father loves to answer yes to. The Lord's Prayer addresses God as *Abba*—the word used by Jewish children for their earthly fathers. Praying to God as "Our Father" conveys the authority, warmth, and intimacy of a loving father's care. "Our Father" is also "in heaven," reminding believers of God's sovereign rule over all things—including the things that we fear the most. And not only that, but our loving and powerful *Abba* wants to and is able to deliver us from evil. An incredible thought!

Of course, the thought of calling God "Father" is not a comforting one for some. Many have experienced not love from their earthly fathers, but abuse. And for those with this experience, to see God through this lens is anything but a comfort. But God is not a God of abuse, and to Him, being *Abba* is to be tender, loving, and protecting. And He is powerful enough to transform your definition of this word—despite the pain you may associate with it.

Because this *Abba* yearns to deliver His children from evil, not subject them to it. And what's more, He is able to do just that for you.

WHAT YOU'LL FIND IN THIS BOOK

If you're reading this and have suffered domestic abuse, we know you must be in the midst of a whirlwind of emotions. So we'll cut to the chase and tell exactly where you can find what you most need to hear:

- If you need to know if what you're experiencing is domestic abuse, please turn to chapter 2.
- If you need to know if others will recognize what you're suffering is considered domestic abuse, please go to chapter 3.
- If you need to know whether you should leave or stay, please turn to chapters 5 and 10.
- If you need to know what he's really thinking and what the obstacles might be to leaving, please turn to chapter 4.
- If you need step-by-step advice on how to get out of an abusive relationship, including supporters to contact, numbers to call, and plans to help you stay safe, please go to appendixes 1 and 2.
- If you are suffering from shame, guilt, and other negative emotions as the result of abuse, please turn to chapter 6.
- If you need to recover from an experience where the words of the Bible have been used to threaten you or keep you in submission, please turn to chapters 7 and 8.
- If you need to know how God views you and your situation, please turn to chapter 9.
- If you need to pray, but don't have the words, please turn to chapter 11.

WHO THIS BOOK IS FOR

Victims and Survivors of Abuse

We use the term "victim" throughout the book, and before we go further we want to explain what we mean. The term "victim" signifies the cruelty and unfairness of domestic violence and puts the responsibility for the assault where it belongs—on the assailant. In this book, we use the term "victim," though "survivor" can also be appropriate as well. Generally, the terms are used interchangeably by people who have experienced domestic violence and by the professionals who interact with them.

However, there are distinctions. "Victim" is often associated with the early trauma following an experience of domestic violence and emphasizes the fact that frequently a crime has been committed. This term is also used for emergency department responses. The terms "survivor" and "victim/survivor" are most often used within later periods of recovery to reclaim power. "Survivor" is often the chosen word for those who do not want to be viewed as remaining under the perpetrator's influence and control.

We will use the term "victim" rather than "survivor" for two reasons. First, the unfortunate reality is that not all victims are survivors as many victims of domestic abuse are killed. Second, some victims do not feel like survivors and using that term can heap shame on them as if they have failed or done something wrong in the healing process. If you prefer the term "survivor," we support you in your chosen identity.

However you identify yourself, please understand this: this book is a resource for healing and hope, not a substitute for reporting abuse, legal care, medical care, counseling, pastoral care, or family and community support. We focus exclusively on the emotional pain resulting from the violence and what the Bible says about the experience of domestic violence. We have ministered to many victims who want and need a clear explanation of how God's grace applies to their experiences of domestic violence and its effects on their lives. We have also talked to many family members, friends, and ministers who know someone who was abused and are looking for a solid, gospel-based book that would be helpful in serving victims.

Pastors, Ministry Leaders, Friends, and Family

If you have tried to approach a church about your experience with abuse and been disappointed, you know firsthand that many churches are woefully underequipped to deal with domestic violence. This is a tragic reality, and one we hope will soon change. But please don't write churches off altogether as a resource for your struggle. Instead, see appendix 3 for ways your local church can care for you if you are at risk.

While this book is primarily for you, it is also for church leaders, church members, and friends and family who know someone in an abusive situation.

If you are a leader in ministry, statistics tell us there are people under your care who have suffered—or are currently suffering—from domestic violence. This is particularly tragic because part of God's mission for the church is to proclaim God's healing and to seek justice for everyone it encounters.[7] And this book is to help equip you in doing just that for women in abusive situations. Additionally, we've put together a list of resources to help further your understanding of domestic violence and how to care for its victims, which you can find in appendix 4.

Women

Finally, we talk about women and use female pronouns for victims. Statistics, which we'll discuss later, point to the fact that the overwhelming majority of domestic violence victims are women. But we also know that there are male victims out there as well, who sometimes suffer from the added burden of feeling that it is unacceptable or a personal failure for a man to be the victim of domestic violence. If you are a man who has been victimized, even though we will focus on women here, please know that you are not forgotten.

A Prayer to Begin

If reading this has sparked the urge to pray, Psalm 55 may be especially apt for you before you read any further. It is a prayer that pleads with God to comfort and save a person who has been harmed by someone close to them. God listens not only to religious psalm writers and holy men from thousands of years ago; He listens to *your* prayers and cries too. Perhaps the words of Psalm 55 can serve as your prayer.

> Listen to my prayer, O God,
>   do not ignore my plea;
>   hear me and answer me . . .
> If an enemy were insulting me,

I could endure it;
if a foe were rising against me,
I could hide.
But it is you, a man like myself,
my companion, my close friend,
with whom I once enjoyed sweet fellowship
at the house of God,
as we walked about
among the worshipers.
Let death take my enemies by surprise;
let them go down alive to the realm of the dead,
for evil finds lodging among them . . .
Evening, morning and noon
I cry out in distress,
and he hears my voice.
(Ps. 55:2–3, 13–15, 17–18)

2

Am I in an Abusive Relationship?

You may already know the answer to this question. But if you don't, it's okay to explore the issue. Either way, we believe you'll soon find you are not alone in your experience.

When the abuse first begins, many women in abusive relationships aren't sure if what they are experiencing is abusive. In fact, one of the biggest hurdles to addressing domestic violence is that very few victims self-identify as experiencing abuse. Many think abuse happens to "those women" and don't want to have the stigma of being one of "those women."

The most telling sign that you are in an abusive relationship is living in fear of your partner. If you feel like you have to walk on eggshells around him—constantly watching what you say and do in order to avoid a blowup—your relationship is unhealthy and likely abusive. Other signs include your partner's belittling of you, his attempts to control you, and feelings of self-loathing, helplessness, and desperation.

An abuser typically has a well-stocked arsenal of ways to exert power over you. He may employ domination, humiliation, isolation, threats, intimidation, denial, blame, and more. What's more, he is often creative and strategic in when—and how—to put these to their most effective use.

None of this is your fault. Your abuser is the only one to blame.

And because he is so good at deceptively wielding control, it can often be difficult to discern if you are being abused. From the perspective of outside observers, these signs of abuse may be cut-and-dry. But

for those trapped in the cycles of abuse, making sense of these complicated relational dynamics—especially when the relationship is intimate—can be suffocating and confusing.

If this is where you find yourself right now, here are some ways to
discern if your relationship is abusive.

SIGNS YOU'RE IN AN ABUSIVE RELATIONSHIP

What the Abuser Does

Some abuse victims may be so confused by the relational dynamics in their relationship—understandably so—that they need to hear
stories and common experiences from others in order to make sense
of their own. Some find it helpful to identify domestic abuse by understanding the common profiles of abusers—and recognizing their
partner among them.

Since abuse is defined by an abuser's behavior—not yours—we'll
start with identifying just that. Here are eight categories or personas
abusers commonly exhibit:[1]

1. Bully
   - Glares
   - Shouts
   - Smashes things
   - Sulks

2. Jailer
   - Stops you from working and seeing friends
   - Tells you what to wear
   - Keeps you in the house
   - Charms your friends or family

3. Headworker
   - Puts you down
   - Tells you you're too fat, too thin, ugly, stupid, useless, etc.

4. Persuader
- Threatens to hurt or kill you or the children
- Cries
- Says he loves you
- Threatens to kill himself
- Threatens to report you to social services

5. Liar
- Denies any abuse
- Says it was "only" a slap
- Blames drinking, drugs, stress, overwork, you, unemployment, etc.

6. Bad Father
- Says you are a bad mother
- Turns the children against you
- Uses access to harass you
- Threatens to take the children away
- Persuades you to have "his" baby and then refuses to help you care for it

7. King of the Castle
- Treats you as a servant/slave
- Says women are for sex, cooking, and housework
- Expects sex on demand[2]
- Controls all the money

8. Sexual Controller
- Sexually assaults you
- Won't accept no for an answer
- Keeps you pregnant
- Rejects your advances and allows sex only when he wants it rather than when you initiate

Next, we'll look at the specific tactics your abuser might use to exert his power and control. The most common tactics include belittling, controlling, and acting violently and/or making violent threats.

YOUR PARTNER'S BELITTLING BEHAVIOR

Does your partner:

- Yell at you?
- Embarrass, insult, criticize you, call you names, or put you down?
- Treat you so badly that you're embarrassed for your family or friends to see?
- Put you down, but then tells you that he loves you?
- Ignore or belittle your opinions or accomplishments?
- Blame you for his abusive behavior?
- Use any mistake you made in the past against you?
- Not allow you to disagree?
- Ignore your feelings and ideas?
- Tell you that you are a bad parent or threaten to take away or hurt your children?
- Act like the abuse is no big deal, tell you it is your fault, or even deny doing it?
- See you as property or a sex object, rather than as a person?

YOUR PARTNER'S CONTROLLING BEHAVIOR

Does your partner:

- Act excessively jealous or possessive?
- Withhold affection as a way to punish you?
- Control where you go, what you do, and demand your whereabouts?
- Keep you from seeing your family or friends?
- Limit your access to money, the phone, or the car?

- Withhold basic necessities (food, clothes, medications, shelter)?
- Make you ask for money or refuse to give you money?
- Restrict you to an allowance?
- Prevent you from working or sabotage your job?
- Steal from you or take your money?
- Constantly check up on you?
- Control your plans and friends?
- Stop you from seeing your family or friends?
- Force you to drop charges?

YOUR PARTNER'S VIOLENT BEHAVIOR OR THREATS

Does your partner:

- Hit, kick, slap, choke, burn, shove, shake, drag, bite, push, punch, or physically harm you in any other way?
- Throw things at you?
- Have a bad and unpredictable temper?
- Threaten to hurt or kill you?
- Threaten to take your children away or harm them?
- Threaten to commit suicide if you leave?
- Intimidate you with guns, knives, or other weapons?
- Destroy your property or belongings?
- Threaten to kill your pet?
- Force, threaten, or coerce you to have sex?
- Destroy your belongings?

The descriptions above are focused on your partner's behavior, which are all telltale signs of abuse. These next questions are for you—to determine how you feel regarding your partner's behavior. The more "yes" answers here, the more likely it is that you're in an abusive relationship.[3]

THE VARIOUS KINDS OF ABUSE

As we've discussed previously, there are different kinds of abuse but all of them are wrong. To help you take inventory of your unique situation, let's consider these different kinds of abuse:

Physical

When we talk about domestic violence, we are often referring to the physical abuse of a spouse or intimate partner. This means using physical force against someone in a way that injures or endangers that person. Physical assault or battering is a crime, whether it occurs inside or outside of the family. The police have the power and authority to protect you from physical attack. And you have the right to protect yourself and your children, if you have them.

Sexual

Any situation in which you are forced to participate in unwanted, unsafe, or degrading sexual activity is sexual abuse. Forced sex, even by a spouse or intimate partner with whom you also have consensual sex, is an act of aggression and violence. Sexual assault includes rape, but it also includes coercion, intimidation, or manipulation to force unwanted sex. We define sexual assault as any type of sexual behavior or contact where consent is not freely given or obtained and is accomplished through force, intimidation, violence, coercion, manipulation, threat, deception, or abuse of authority.[4]

Sexual assault is a display of power by the perpetrator against the victim. It is not a product of an "uncontrollable" sexual urge. In fact, it is not actually about sex at all; it is about violence and control. Perpetrators use sexual actions and behaviors as weapons to dominate, control, and belittle another person.

If you feel as though you are being pressured into sex or that you are doing something that you do not want in order to placate your partner, then let us tell you now that your feelings are valid and that it is abuse.

As shaming as sexual assault feels, you aren't alone in this either.

According to surveys, one in four women will be sexually assaulted at some point in their lifetimes, and these statistics are probably underestimates.[5] Sexual assault can occur in marriage. As a matter of fact, researchers have estimated that sexual assault occurs in 10–14% of all marriages.[6]

Emotional

Most people can identify physical abuse—pushing, hitting, kicking—if it is happening in their relationship. Emotional abuse, on the other hand, is not always so easily spotted.

It's harder to pinpoint exactly what's wrong, and easier to minimize what's really going on. It doesn't leave you bleeding or bruised. The neighbors can't hear it (not always) through the walls. But emotional abuse is no less destructive than physical abuse, and it is no less wrong.

The aim of emotional abuse is to chip away at your feelings of self-worth and independence—a violent process, in that it degrades you and your sense of your God-given worth. If you're the victim of emotional abuse, you may feel that there is no way out of the relationship, or that without your abusive partner you will have nothing.

So how *can* you identify if what you're experiencing is emotional abuse? There are several ways. Emotional abuse includes *verbal abuse* such as yelling, name-calling, blaming, and shaming. Isolation, intimidation, and controlling behavior are also signs of emotional abuse. Sometimes, abusers throw in threats of physical violence or other repercussions if you don't do what they want.

Emotional abuse also includes *economic abuse* such as withholding money and basic necessities, restricting you to an allowance, sabotaging your job, and stealing from you or taking your money.

These are just some examples. But if you don't see your particular experience listed here, use this as a general guide: Does your partner do something deliberately and repeatedly that puts you down or thwarts your plans? If the person who is supposed to be providing love, support, and guidance is keeping you in a situation where you are constantly made to feel inferior, you aren't in a healthy relationship.

REFLECTING ON YOUR PARTNER'S BEHAVIOR

Reflect on your partner's abusive behavior. Do you see him in these pages? Can you see evidence that the behaviors were deliberate, controlled, or planned? Does he act differently toward you when there are other people around? How has he attempted to stop your resistance to his abuse? Does he treat others with respect, while treating you with disrespect?

In chapter 3, we'll explore some of the reasons why he chooses to abuse. But first, let's take a look at your own experience to get clarity on your situation. Our hope is that as we spell out the nuances of what you may be experiencing, you will be able to call it what it is, plain and simple—abuse.

YOUR THOUGHTS AND FEELINGS

Do you:

- Feel afraid of your partner most of the time?
- Avoid certain topics out of fear of angering your partner?
- Feel afraid of your partner's temper?
- Feel afraid to disagree?
- Feel that you can't do anything right for your partner?
- Believe you deserve to be hurt or mistreated?
- Have to justify everything you do, every place you go, or every person you talk to in order to avoid your partner's anger?
- Feel afraid to leave or break up because your partner has threatened to hurt you, himself, or someone else?
- Avoid seeing family or friends because of your partner's jealousy?
- Wonder if you're the one who is crazy?
- Feel emotionally numb or helpless?

IT IS STILL ABUSE IF . . .

A handbook for victims of violence, *Breaking the Silence*, makes these important points about abuse:[7]

It is still abuse if . . .

- The incidents of physical abuse seem minor when compared to those you have read about, seen on television, or heard other women talk about. There isn't a "better" or "worse" form of physical abuse; any physical harm is a serious offense.
- The incidents of physical abuse have only occurred one or two times in the relationship. Studies indicate that if your spouse/partner has injured you once, it is likely he will do it again.
- The physical assaults stopped when you became passive and gave up your right to express yourself as you desire, to move about freely and see others, and to make decisions. It is not a victory if you have to give up your rights as a person and a partner in exchange for not being assaulted!
- There has not been any physical violence. Many women are emotionally and verbally assaulted. This can be as equally frightening and is often more confusing to try to understand.

THE POWER AND CONTROL WHEEL

Domestic violence is about exerting power and control. As Ann Jones and Susan Schecter explain, "What matters to the controller is not what he does but what he gains by doing it."[8]

The following "Power and Control Wheel"[9] can be helpful for you to evaluate where you stand in your relationship. It identifies aspects of abusive behavior and its underlying motivation as emotional power and control. The wheel is a tool created by researchers to help define and identify *some* of the behaviors used to maintain power and control. So if you don't see an exact description here of what you're going through, don't jump to the conclusion that what you are experiencing isn't abuse.

Abusers may begin with physical or sexual abuse—the outer rim—to help establish the control. Once established, physical and sexual abuse may no longer be used to maintain the emotional control. A look or tone from the abuser may serve to control the victim once abuse has been established in the relationship. However, the pattern in some cases is reversed—some abusers begin with the inner spokes and escalate to physical or sexual abuse when the behaviors listed on the inside are no longer effective for them to maintain power and control.

Anne Ganley, a therapist in Seattle who writes on healing from abuse, uses the distinction between "hands-on" and "hands-off" abuse.[10] Hands-on includes physical and sexual abuse. Hands-off involves psychological, verbal, and emotional abuse. This includes threats (such as suicide, removing the children, hurting the children, deportation),

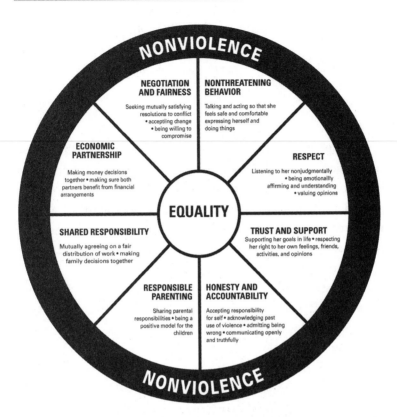

forcing the victim to perform degrading acts (eating dinner out of the dog bowl, eating cigarettes left in an ashtray, licking the kitchen or bathroom floor), controlling the victim's activities (such as sleeping and eating habits, relationships, access to money), attacking the victim's self-esteem, denying the validity of her feelings and ideas, or intentionally frightening the victim.

The "Power and Control Wheel" shows the vast amount of ways that abusers exert power and control over their intimate partners. Many women do not realize the different ways that an abuser has been harming them until they are out and away from his grip of power and control. So we've included another tool to figure out if you are in an abusive relationship: the "Equality Wheel," which was developed to describe a nonviolent, non-abusive partnership. This wheel represents healthy or ideal behaviors that one would hope to find in a relationship. The core of a healthy relationship focuses on equality. Once a power imbalance has occurred in a relationship, it opens the door for abusive behavior.

THE CYCLE OF ABUSE

The specifics of domestic violence differ from situation to situation, but domestic violence tends to follow a pattern no matter when it occurs or who is involved. The pattern or cycle repeats and can happen many times during a relationship. This may be difficult to read about if this pattern is a reality in your life rather than words on a page, but we hope that by describing the pattern, you will get a clear picture of the depth of the situation.

The pattern starts at its center, which is the abuser himself. He puts his wants and whims first and foremost. And while the abuser's life revolves around what he wants, the life of the abused revolves around the abuser.

Every morning, the guessing game begins anew. *What mood will he be in today? What precautions can I take to avoid hidden minefields? What will happen if I upset him again?*

This leads the victim to be very careful of what she says, how she responds, her facial expressions, and even how she dresses. The victim has oriented her whole existence to please him, and their happiness and peace depends on his moods and how he feels about everything. The victim works to keep the peace.

The pattern of domestic violence may be best understood through several phases. Each phase may last a different length of time and over time the level of violence may increase. And remember, not all domestic violence relationships fit the cycle and not everyone's experiences are the same.

The cycle of violence is a tool developed by researcher Lenore Walker in her book *The Battered Woman Syndrome*.[11] On average, about one-third of domestic violence victims can identify with this cycle. Examining the cycle of violence reveals the complexity of abuse and how abusers can skillfully blend abuse with loving behaviors.

If you aren't sure if you can break things off, or if you think that the cycle will naturally be broken if you leave, it's important to see the whole picture and to understand what he might do in response. As you will see, the worst parts will always subside if he doesn't think it's an effective way to keep you in his power, but when he has lured you back, nothing will have changed. And without intervention, the frequency and severity of the abuse tends to increase—spiraling downward in the cycle of abuse.

The cycle below describes the main phases of abusive incidents in more detail so that you can see which ones might apply to your particular situation.

TENSION PHASE

During the tension phase, the victim often feels like they are walking on eggshells. This phase may last for weeks or even months, and in it:

- Stress begins to build
- Communication breaks down
- The victim senses growing danger, and tries to avoid it
- Violence/abuse occurs, yet the victim perceives it as "minor"
- Incidents occur more often, intensity increases
- Family denies, minimizes, blames external factors
- The victim begins to hope "somehow" things will change

CRISIS PHASE

The crisis phase is easily recognizable, because in it, the abuser often simply snaps. This phase may last anywhere from two hours to 24 hours, or even span over several days. In the crisis phase:

- The victim's anxiety runs extremely high
- Major, uncontrolled violence occurs

- The abuse becomes explosive, acute, and unpredictable
- The abuse may result in serious injuries, even death
- The abuser blames the victim
- The victim accommodates in order to survive
- The victim may escape during this phase, yet often returns when the crisis is over
- The victim may isolate herself and collapse emotionally

CALM PHASE

This phase is exactly what it sounds like—the calm after the storm. This is when the abuser often showers the victim with apologies and false promises. The calm phase may last for days or weeks, and in it:

- The whole family is in shock at first
- The abuser may be extremely remorseful and seek forgiveness
- All are relieved that crisis is past
- The victim is worn down, accepts promises, presents
- Children become caretakers to "keep the peace"
- The abuser may display kind, loving behavior
- The family welcomes this "honeymoon" stage and wants to believe violence won't recur

THE CYCLE FROM THE PERSPECTIVE OF THE ABUSER

This is the experience of the cycle from your point of view. Now here is what the cycle looks like within the mind of the abuser:

- Abuse—Your abusive partner lashes out with aggressive, belittling, or violent behavior. The abuse is a power play designed to show you "who is boss."
- Guilt—After abusing you, your partner feels guilt but not over what he's done. He's more worried about the possibility of being caught and facing consequences for his abusive behavior.
- Excuses—To sidestep this guilt, your abuser rationalizes what

he has done. The person may come up with a string of excuses or blame you for the abusive behavior—anything to avoid taking responsibility.

- "Normal" behavior—The abuser does everything he can to regain control and keep the victim in the relationship. He may act as if nothing has happened, or he may turn on the charm. This peaceful "honeymoon" phase may give the victim hope that the abuser has really changed this time.

- Fantasy and planning—But then your abuser begins to fantasize about abusing you again. He spends a lot of time thinking about what you've done wrong and how he'll make you pay. Then he makes a plan for turning the fantasy of abuse into reality.

- Setup—Your abuser sets you up and puts his plan in motion. What's more, by now he's convinced himself that he is perfectly justified in punishing you in this way.

The abuser's apologies and affectionate gestures in between the episodes of abuse can make it difficult to leave. He may make you believe that you are the only person who can help him, that things will be different this time, and that he truly loves you. However, the dangers of staying are very real—as you will experience anew every time the cycle starts all over again.

Here's an example of a full cycle of domestic violence looking from the outside in: A man abuses his partner. After he hurts her, he experiences self-directed guilt. He says, "I'm sorry for hurting you." What he does not say is, "Because I might get caught." He then rationalizes his behavior by saying that his partner is having an affair with someone. He tells her, "If you weren't such a worthless whore, I wouldn't have to hurt you." He then acts contrite, reassuring her that he will not hurt her again. He then fantasizes and reflects on past abuse and how he will hurt her again. He plans on telling her to go to the store to get some groceries. What he withholds from her is that she only has a certain amount of time to do the shopping. When she is held up in traffic and is a few minutes late, he feels completely justified in abusing her because, "You're having an affair with the store clerk." He has just set her up.[12]

TREE, TRUNK, AND ROOTS

Lundy Bancroft, a consultant who has studied extensively the minds of abusive men, writes, "Abuse grows from attitudes and values, not feelings. The roots are ownership, the trunk is entitlement, and the branches are control."[13] The issue of abuse is not only about having control of and power over someone else. The abuser uses power and control as tools to support his belief that he owns his wife or partner and that he is entitled to certain treatment.

This is why violence against women increases in cultures and countries where women are actually owned (through practices of dowry) and where issues of male entitlement run higher (e.g., machismo culture). It also explains why most abusers are male—and most victims, female—because male ownership and entitlement runs through the root of almost all societies. We would suggest that this is because male domination was a primary consequence of the fall. In Genesis 3:16, after the fall, God responds to Eve, saying: "Your desire will be for your husband, and he will rule over you." This does not mean God determined men should rule their wives—that male domination is ideal and how it should be. Rather, we see this man's ruling over his wife as a consequence of sin—that is *not* the best plan for humanity. This is further evidenced by the fact that before the fall, men and women were equal.

Chauvinism and misogyny are effects of sin; they are not part of God's design for men and women. Chauvinism says that men and women have been created in a hierarchy with the male as the higher, superior sex—much like a king born into a family with a natural right to exercise authority over the rest of his nation. Chauvinism upholds that women, in contrast, are the weaker or lesser of the sexes, inheriting a natural role of submission to the man—like the citizens of a country who have no natural claim to authority.

But we don't believe that God created you to be in this role.

The practical implication of chauvinism is that in the family, the church, and in society at large, women are not to exercise authority over men because it's believed that they are incapable of doing so by virtue of how they have been made.

This is the assumption of "male privilege," which is a term that refers generally to the special rights or status granted to men but denied to women in a society on the basis of their sex. This position is very problematic because it's oppressive. And it can often, tragically, become the foundation of abuse. Moreover, this position misunderstands God's creative intentions for men and women.

In other words, we believe abuse is not just a case-by-case incident. It is an epidemic—and since we are Christians, we believe that it is an outgrowth of the human sinfulness. Abuse is not the way things should be. You were made for more than this.

3

Why Does He Choose to Abuse?

The first question faced by victims of abuse is often: *Am I in an abusive relationship?* And when this question has been answered, it stirs up a second question of equal importance: *Is the abuse my fault?*

We understand you may wonder if things might improve if only you were a bit more compliant, or if you had a stronger backbone, or maybe if you simply stayed out of his way. But research tells another story, and it is one you need to know.

Research on domestic violence reveals that a woman's behavior actually has no bearing on the abuse. In fact, all of the factors that lead to increased or decreased violence are characteristics of the abuser, not the victim. Psychologists Neil Jacobson and John Gottman say it plainly: "There was nothing battered women could do to stop the abuse except get out of the relationship."[1]

Ultimately, abusive men do not abuse because of what their partners do or do not do; they abuse because of complex internal pathologies beyond your control or responsibility.[2]

In other words, and as we have said before, *it is not your fault*.

The abuser is the only one to blame for his abuse. Of course, he does not want you to see it this way. As we have discussed, men who abuse share some common characteristics—and one of these characteristics is to blame-shift. They want you to believe that you are at fault for the abuse you are receiving. But this is not true.

Focusing on your abuser's behavior—rather than your response to his behavior—is crucial for you to get past any feelings of guilt for what has happened to you. The question of "Why don't you leave?" is an important one, but is often used to put the responsibility on you—

the one experiencing abuse. Our hope is that people will instead begin asking "Why does he choose to abuse?"

ABUSIVE MEN CHOOSE TO ABUSE

While characteristics vary from person to person, all abusers share one thing in common: they choose to abuse deliberately.

They may blame their behavior on you, an abusive childhood, stress, alcohol problems, their cultural background, financial problems, or their personalities.

Others aid in this false claim by assuming violence and abuse only happen because the abuser isn't able to control his behavior. Others still believe abusers do what they do because they were abused as a child, or that their behavior is dictated by mental illness. Certainly childhood issues, alcohol, drugs, mental, and other health problems may be factors of domestic abuse, but they are not the cause.

The truth is, the only reason an abuser abuses is because he chooses to. Contrary to what some believe, abusers *are* able to control their behavior—they do it all the time. Just look at how they behave when they are not around their victims.

The flip side of this is that if abusers can indeed control their actions, we believe that perpetrators can also choose to behave respectfully toward others. The bottom line is, whether he chooses to abuse or to respect, the responsibility for his choice is his alone. And yet, it is not worth risking your safety to stay around and find out what he will choose.

We know that certain factors intensify an abuser's desire to abuse, but none of those factors cause abuse. Abusers abuse for one reason: because they want to. Yet there are no acceptable reasons for a partner to abuse another in an intimate relationship.

Here's why we believe he's in control of what he's doing. Have you ever seen him suddenly change his behavior in the middle of an abusive episode? Have you noticed that he does not abuse others—only you or your children? More than that, an abuser often makes strategic decisions about the type and amount of abuse. Perpetrators have rules about how far they will go. They are selective about where they will inflict injury on a victim's body—for example, where the bruises will not be seen in public. Many abusers are also excellent at concealing their violent tendencies, putting on a charming face in public and waiting to unleash their anger and abuse only in the privacy of their own home. All of this shows abusers are quite purposeful about how and where they choose to abuse.

So if abuse is always his fault, why do women stay?

WHY SOME ABUSED WOMEN STAY

There are lots of reasons why a person might choose to stay in an abusive relationship. Staying doesn't mean that you like the abuse or that it cannot be "that bad." No matter why you stay, the abuse is never your fault. We know that the deck is stacked against you when confronted with leaving or not. There is a very real fear of retaliation or even death if you leave, but as we will talk about later, we believe leaving is a risk well worth taking.

While we urge you to leave as soon as possible, we know there are a variety of factors why you might be staying with an abuser or have not yet left. Combining the insights of theology, sociology, and therapy, Catherine Clark Kroeger, Nancy Nason-Clark, and Helene L. Conway offer numerous reasons why women do not leave or end a violent relationship:[3]

- Fear is the number one reason women do not leave abusive husbands and violent homes. An abused woman fears for her future, fears further violence, and fears for the lives of her children. Fear permeates her life and is often experienced as a paralyzing terror, ruling her day and destroying her sleep through nightmares.
- Finances—economic dependency—keep many women from perceiving that there are options besides life with their violent

partner. A woman's lack of personal or economic resources, coupled with the fact that she might never have been employed, means she cannot see the alternatives.

- The fantasy of change, or the hope that someday the violence will cease, keeps many women with violent husbands for years or for a lifetime.
- Afraid that no one will believe them. Sometimes victims stay because they are afraid that no one will believe them. Often an abuser will use this as a threat to keep the victim in the relationship.
- Low self-esteem. Experiencing abuse can erode a person's self-esteem. They may find it difficult to make decisions or think clearly during this time.
- Mixed feelings. The victim may have mixed feelings for the abuser. They may be torn between the abuser's "good qualities" and wanting the abuse to end.
- Religious or cultural beliefs can affect their acceptance of abuse. The victim's religion or culture may condone some forms of relationship violence.
- Religious beliefs sometimes cause women to feel that God does not permit them to leave, that marriage is forever, that this is their cross to bear, or that perpetual forgiveness of their husband for his repeated behavior is God's expectation. Religious women are especially likely to cling to the belief that their violent husband wants to and will change his behavior. Here it is critical that the victim seek out wise counsel from a trained pastor and counselor to help her navigate these issues.
- Cultural pressures may keep a victim from leaving her abuser. The victim may feel pressure from family, friends, and/or society to stay in the relationship and not give up, even if their partner is abusive.
- Children in the picture can often cause a victim to reconsider leaving when she weighs the emotional, financial, and educa-

tional consequences of taking the children away from their father. A mother may feel that her children are better off at home especially if the abuser is not directly violent to the children.

- Other emotions, such as shame of a failed relationship or embarrassment at the intimate nature of her horrors, may make a victim reluctant to leave since she knows she will have to explain her reasons for leaving to others.
- The abuser may have made threats to the victim about leaving. Threats can range from physical threats to the victim or someone the victim cares about, to suicide, and even blackmail. The victim may feel trapped.
- The victim may have tried to break up with the abuser in the past only to be abused with more intensity or stalked by him.

THE RESISTANCE OF ABUSED WOMEN

Those who have been abused are often actively resisting their abusers, but all too often, their resistance goes unnoticed by outsiders. Family and friends may assume that victims have not done enough to protect themselves and have created their own misfortunes. Also, victims tend not to talk about their experiences of abuse to stay safer from the perpetrator, and to avoid the negative judgments of others. Often family, friends, and professionals do not hear the full story of how much victims have suffered or how much they have resisted the abuse. If you've been abused and have resisted your abuser, sadly, you're likely to have experienced at least some of what is mentioned above. This experience is often painful and embarrassing.

You may experience messages from others that leave you feeling shameful and disheartened. Acquaintances may imply that you're "damaged" or even "responsible" for the abuse. Well-meaning family and friends may feel there is something wrong with you for having picked an abuser to marry, or believe you are so damaged that you are likely going to pick another abuser.

Too often women who resist abuse are seen to be at fault when they resist or stand up to the abuser. However, if you've resisted your abuser, you're showing that you've maintained something of your humanity and self-esteem in the face of horrendous abuse. If this is you, you should be supported, celebrated, assisted, and encouraged—not blamed, offered platitudes, asked suspicious questions, and told bad theology.

Some people make an assumption that victims passively accept violence, and lack self-esteem, assertiveness, or boundaries. But all victims do things to oppose abuse and to keep their dignity. No victim wants to be abused, and they do resist it in some way. They do stand up against, refuse to comply with, and try to stop or prevent violence, disrespect, and oppression.

Of course, abuse is dangerous territory, so usually victims resist it in small and subtle ways. Others may not even notice the resistance so they assume that victims are "passive" and "they do not do enough to stand up for themselves." In fact, victims actively resist violence.

About this, advocates of domestic abuse explain, "It is not surprising that many victims are also confused about their partner's violent behavior, and do not understand why he does such mean and hurtful things. In our view, this 'failure to understand' is another way that victims resist abuse. It shows that victims know there are no acceptable reasons for abusive behavior."[4]

Society may look at you in your situation and cast blame for staying. And while we do believe staying puts you at personal risk, we also believe that by even acknowledging what you are experiencing as abuse—which is without excuse—shows tremendous courage.

In appendix 2, we have listed some tips on who to talk to and how to plan a safe exit strategy. But in the meantime, we want you to know that simply by acknowledging that this abuse is a problem in your relationship, you've done something extraordinary.

4

What Is Domestic Violence?

B ecause the last things abusers want is for their victims to identify their experience as "domestic violence," it can often be very difficult to do so. Maybe you feel afraid, ashamed, guilty, angry, confused, helpless, hopeless, drained, depressed, and frightened—but you don't know what to name what is happening to you. You may also feel very alone in your experience. But we want you to know how common your experience is. What we plan to do here is to give you a sense of how laws define domestic violence (it's broader than you think!) and to show you how prevalent it is in our society. The statistics are staggering, but we want you to recognize that you are not alone in what you are going through and there are many others who understand.

DEFINING DOMESTIC VIOLENCE

Domestic violence is used as an overarching term to encompass a large number of behaviors—physical, verbal, and psychological—that violate the well-being of an individual and his or her ability to act. There is currently little consensus among practitioners and researchers on which term to use—domestic violence or intimate partner violence—and how to define those terms exactly. What's more, they may be defined differently in medical, legal, political, or social contexts. But the point is, the legal definition of all that constitutes domestic violence is a wide one.

In general, these terms mean the same thing. Intimate partner violence is used to describe abuse between current or former "romantic" partners. Domestic violence can include abuse from a household member such as a roommate or caretaker, intimate partners, or a family member—whether or not they live with the victim. For this book, our focus is on domestic violence between only intimate partners, though many principles widely apply to other forms of domestic violence. In this book, we've also decided to use the more common and well-known term "domestic violence" but are comfortable with "intimate partner violence" or "intimate partner abuse."[1] See the note for a fuller explanation of these terms.

Historically, "domestic violence" was mostly associated with physical violence. "Domestic violence" today, however, has a much broader legal definition, which includes sexual, psychological, verbal, and economic abuse.[2] So if you are wondering if your situation is serious enough to be classified as abuse, the courts are probably more sympathetic than you might think.

A NARROW AND BROAD UNDERSTANDING

The purpose of defining domestic violence is twofold. Of course, you first need to be able to define it for yourself and to name what you are experiencing. Second, you need to be able to talk about your experience with those who haven't had to live in an abusive situation themselves.

We are going to give a general definition here. Let's start by discussing what violence is, in terms everybody can agree upon: "Violence is the extreme application of social control. Usually understood as the use of physical force, it can take a psychological form when manifested through direct harassment or implied terroristic threats. Violence can also be structural, as when institutional forces such as governments or medical systems impinge upon individuals' rights to bodily integrity, or contribute to the deprivation of basic human needs."[3] Many persons understand violence in primarily physical terms—something that harms the body. As this definition makes clear, more and more people are recognizing that using force to control someone at any level (psychological, emotional, sexual, etc.) is violence just the same.[4]

Our definition of domestic violence favors the broader view.

Domestic violence is a pattern of coercive, controlling, or abusive behavior that is used by one individual to gain or maintain power and control over another individual in the context of an intimate relationship. This includes any behaviors that frighten, intimidate, terrorize, exploit, manipulate, hurt, humiliate, blame, injure, or wound an intimate partner. If you take a minute to look at our reference notes, you'll realize this definition isn't just our personal preference. It's the increasing consensus of psychologists, lawmakers, and experts in the field (partly for that reason, this section will sound a little more clinical).

As such, domestic violence can take many forms, including willful intimidation, physical assault,[5] sexual assault, battery, stalking,[6] verbal abuse,[7] emotional abuse, economic control,[8] psychological abuse, spiritual abuse, isolation, any other abusive behavior, and/or threats of such. Of course, threats of abuse can be as frightening as the abuse itself, particularly, when the victim knows the perpetrator may carry out the threats.

Former or current spouses, opposite-sex cohabitating partners, same-sex cohabitating partners, boyfriends, girlfriends, ex-boyfriends, ex-girlfriends, and dates can commit domestic violence. For the purpose of this book, "intimate partner relationship" is defined as a relationship between two people who may or may not be married, heterosexual, homosexual, living together (cohabitating), dating, separated, divorced, or currently in a relationship.[9]

Intimate violence includes the establishment of abusive control and power over another person through fear, isolation, and/or intimidation.[10] Violent behavior, such as the act of engaging in intimate violence, often is thought of as direct "hands-on" infliction of pain but also includes implied threat or actual physical, sexual, and emotional abuse, including withholding finances and medical equipment.[11]

This understanding of domestic violence gets beyond our society's narrow understanding of the issue and expands the spectrum of actions to be considered domestic violence. Our comprehensive definition and understanding of domestic violence includes several elements. Each element is important in understanding domestic violence:

- *Intentional:* The abuser consciously or subconsciously sets out to use deliberate abusive tactics to achieve his/her ends. The abuser chooses to abuse and he can choose to stop abusing at any time.
- *Methodical:* The abuser systematically uses a series of abusive tactics to gain power over the partner and to control her.
- *Pattern:* The abused partner often at first sees the abusive tactics as isolated and unrelated incidents, but they are really a series of related acts that form a pattern of behaviors.
- *Tactics:* The abuser uses a variety of tactics to gain power and to control his partner such as threats, violence, humiliation, exploitation, or even self-pity.
- *Power:* The abuser aims to acquire and employ power in the relationship. For example, the abuser may use force or threats of physical harm to intimidate his or her partner, thereby gaining physical and emotional power. Or the abuser may prohibit the partner from working, making the partner financially dependent on the abuser, and thereby gaining financial power.
- *Control:* With sufficient power, the abuser can control his partner—forcing or coercing her to do as the abuser wishes. For example, the abuser controls the decision making for the relationship, or controls who has social contact with the partner, or determines the sexual practices of the partner. The goal of the abuser is to force compliance.
- *Desires:* The abuser's ultimate goal is to get his emotional and physical desires met and he aims to selfishly make use of his partner to meet those needs. Most abusers are afraid their desires will not be fulfilled through a normal healthy relationship. Fear motivates them to use abuse to ensure that their desires will be met.

Domestic violence is a pervasive, life-threatening epidemic and crime that affects millions of people worldwide in every community.

It takes place across all races, ages, socioeconomic statuses, geographic regions, religions, nationalities, and education backgrounds, including traditional, nontraditional, teen dating, and adult dating relationships as well as older populations.[12] You are not alone.

A NATIONAL PROBLEM

Domestic violence is dangerously good at hiding itself, yet it is extremely prevalent—and extremely damaging—in our world today.

Domestic violence exists in every community and culture (including communities and cultures that we might perceive as happy and "normal"). The number of occurrences of domestic violence is staggering. Around the world, at least one in every three women has been beaten, coerced into sex, or otherwise abused at some point during her lifetime. Most often, the abuser is a member of her own family.

Intimate partner violence is pervasive in U.S. society. The prevalence of domestic violence in the United States is difficult to determine because the crime is vastly underreported, yet the statistics are still overwhelmingly high: one in every four women will experience domestic violence in her lifetime.[13] Statistics about domestic violence are based on reported acts, with between two to four million women being abused physically by an intimate partner each year in the U.S.[14] Women of all races are about equally vulnerable to violence by an intimate partner.

Pastor and social activist Ron Clark puts it into perspective this way:

If our nation were a church of 400 people, one could estimate that 160 would be adult women, twenty would be teenage girls, 160 would be adult men, and twenty would be teenage boys. According to national statistics, forty of the women would experience some form of physical abuse in their life. Twenty of the women would be currently experiencing physical abuse. Four of five of the teenage girls would experience some type of dating violence. If abuse is expanded to include verbal and emotional abuse, then at least eighty of the women would be experiencing the humiliation and degradation of verbal criticism from a spouse or boyfriend. Approximately sixty of the men and boys would have assaulted their girlfriend or wife at some time. It could also be expected that half of the congregation (200 people) would have witnessed abuse in their family or their spouse's family and 150 of them would have known of a woman who has been abused in the past year. Even more than this, some of the men and boys in the congregation would be actively abusing some of the women.[15]

Nearly three out of four (74%) of Americans personally know someone who is or has been a victim of domestic violence. Approximately 30% of Americans say they know a woman who has been physically abused by her husband or boyfriend in the past year.[16] So if you haven't told anyone about your abuse, remember that even if it seems as though the situation is isolating, many of the people you talk to already know others with a similar experience.

In terms of lifetime abuse rates, various studies show that 22–33% of American women will be assaulted—including rape, physical violence, or stalking—by an intimate partner in their lifetimes.[17] A 2001 U.S. study revealed that 85% of the victims were female with a male abuser.[18] Historically, females have been most often victimized by someone they knew.[19] The other 15% includes intimate partner violence in gay and lesbian relationships and men who were abused by a female partner.[20] Women are 90–95% more likely to suffer domestic violence than men.[21] Women living with female intimate partners experience less intimate partner violence than women living with male intimate partners. Men living with male intimate partners experience more intimate partner violence than do men who live with female intimate partners.[22] These findings provide further evidence that intimate partner violence is perpetrated primarily by men, whether against male or female partners. The numbers show that overall, women are at far greater risk of intimate partner violence than are men.[23]

Young women are particularly at risk. Women between the ages of 16 and 24 experience the highest rate of intimate partner violence and sexual assault.[24] Similarly, women who are 20–24 years of age are at the greatest risk of nonfatal intimate partner violence.[25] And among teenage girls, one in three reports knowing a friend or a peer who has been hit, punched, kicked, slapped, or physically injured by a partner.[26]

Violence against women is primarily intimate partner violence: 64% of women who reported being raped, physically assaulted, and/ or stalked since the age of 18 were victimized by a current or former husband, cohabitating partner, boyfriend, or date.[27]

CHILDREN

Even if the recipient of abuse is the mother (and not any children), children are affected by domestic abuse in staggering and long-lasting ways. And it is here, among some of the household's most vulnerable members, that we see some of the most toxic effects of the cycle of abuse. If you have children, this section will be especially hard to read, but please bear with us, because we think it's important that you know this information.

To begin with, studies suggest that between 10–15 million children are exposed to domestic violence every year.[28] And for these children, abusive adults can cause tremendous long-term physical, emotional, and spiritual damage in their lives. This is true even if they physically abuse the mother (but the children are not physically hurt), though roughly half of men who physically abuse their wives also abuse their children.[29] Bruce Perry, one of the top neurological trauma researchers in the world, has conclusively shown that when young children merely witness domestic violence, this trauma exposure creates long-term physiological changes, including significant structural alteration and damage to the brain.[30]

The aftermath of abuse comes out in children's behavior as well. Children exposed to violence are more likely to attempt suicide, abuse drugs and alcohol, run away from home, be exploited in teenage prostitution, and commit sexual assault crimes.[31] Children who witness violence at home display emotional and behavioral disturbances as diverse as withdrawal, low self-esteem, nightmares, self-blame, and aggression against peers, family members, and property.[32]

The damage also occurs in more intangible ways. Children who witness the abuse often experience their mother's powerlessness and humiliation. Many lose their childhood innocence because their sense of security has been violated and they feel dramatically unsafe. Children often develop anxiety in anticipation of the next attack, blame themselves for the abuse, and fear abandonment—especially if they should fail to keep the violence secret. They are left isolated and frightened as they carry the weight of shame, responsibility, guilt, and anger.[33]

And here, among children, we see one of the most toxic effects of the cycle of abuse: Witnessing violence from one parent or caregiver to another is the strongest risk factor of transmitting violent behavior from one generation to the next.[34] Boys who witness domestic violence are *twice as likely* to abuse their own partners and children when they become adults.[35] Men exposed to physical abuse, sexual abuse, and/or domestic violence as children are almost four times more likely than other men to perpetrate domestic violence as adults.[36]

The most common factor among men who abuse their wives is that they experienced (received or witnessed) domestic violence themselves in childhood. Again, this history does not excuse anyone from choosing destructive behavior, but it does illustrate the far-reaching effects of abuse.

Additionally, we know that girls who grow up in physically abusive homes are more likely to be physically and sexually victimized by their own intimate partners in adulthood. Daughters are more than six times more likely to be sexually abused in homes where intimate partner violence occurs.[37] Children in homes where domestic violence occurs are physically abused or seriously neglected at a rate of 1500% higher than the national average in the general population.[38] And even when they grow into adults, children who've grown up in abusive households are

15 times more likely to be abused by other adults.

If you are reading this and are still on the fence about getting out of the relationship. All of these studies point to destructive effects of abuse that are long-term. Even if your child has not personally suffered abuse yet, the consequences of even witnessing it in the home over the rest of their lives could be catastrophic.

FREQUENCY AND DURATION

One of the common perceptions that keep many women in abusive relationships is the belief that this time, he'll change—that this time, he really means it when he says it won't happen again. But the numbers tell another story.

According to the U.S. Department of Justice, approximately half of the women raped by an intimate partner and two-thirds of the women physically assaulted by an intimate partner said they were victimized multiple times by the same partner.[39] Female rape victims have reported 4.5 rapes on average by the same partner, and female physical assault victims averaged 6.9 assaults. Among women who were victimized multiple times by the same partner, 63% of rape victims and 70% of assault victims say their victimization lasted a year or more. On average, women who were raped multiple times said their victimization occurred over 3.8 years, and women who were physically assaulted multiple times said their victimization occurred over 4.5 years.[40]

Your abuser may say it won't happen again, but more often than not, it will. This is a difficult truth to come to terms with, but we believe it is important for you to know for your own safety.

THE REALITY OF LEAVING

You are the expert for your situation; what we are telling you may be new information, but we know you will have been doing everything you can to manage yourself and any children involved. An abuser will attempt to totally disempower you and force you to stop trusting your own instincts. We would encourage you to begin trusting your own instincts and when possible seek help. You will already be taking steps to keep yourself and any children safe. Using the resources in appendix 2, this risk can be dramatically decreased through taking certain steps and accessing specialist support. All of the studies and statistics we have discussed here point to long-lasting damage if you stay, but we also want to be clear about the risks of leaving.

To begin with, domestic abuse does not end immediately with separation from the abuser. We believe leaving is a critical step for a woman in an abusive relationship, but as critical as it is, it is also dangerous. Over 75% of separated women suffer post-separation abuse.[41] Not only that, but even if the separation seems at first successful, there is an ongoing risk to a person once they leave an abusive relationship.

The abuser may begin to stalk and harass the woman once she has left. And then there is the emotional impact that surfaces when someone is finally out from under the abuse. However, this is also the time when the emotional support from family and friends often stops. This is why it is important to remind supporters to stick around. Approximately 75% of all domestic homicides occur while the victim is trying to leave their abuser or has just left the relationship.[42] This is a valid fear, and if you believe you may be at risk, skip down to the section, "Reporting and Protection Orders."

To keep yourself and your children safe, please review the following risk factors. It is important to note that the presence of a risk factor does not mean that violent behavior will necessarily occur, only that the odds of it occurring are greater. These risks include the following:

- Unmarried, cohabiting couples have higher rates of intimate partner violence than do married couples. Unmarried couples are at greater risk of intimate partner violence than married couples.[43]
- Minorities have higher rates of intimate partner violence than do white people.[44]

- Lower income women have higher rates of intimate partner violence than do higher income women.[45]
- Less educated women have higher rates of intimate partner violence than do more educated women.[46]
- Couples with income, educational, or occupational status disparities have higher rates of intimate partner violence than do couples with no status disparity.[47]
- Women were significantly more likely to report violence by a current partner if their education level was greater than their partner's.
- Experiencing and/or witnessing violence in one's family of origin increases one's chances of being a perpetrator or victim of intimate partner violence.[48]
- Wife assault is more common in families where power is concentrated in the hands of the husband or male partner and the husband makes most of the decisions regarding family finances and strictly controls when and where his wife or female partner goes.[49]
- Persons with a disability are at greater risk of violence,[50] although there is no empirical evidence that having a disability increases one's risk of intimate partner violence.

Verbal abuse is one of the biggest indicators that physical abuse may follow. Much of the violence perpetrated against women by male partners is part of a systematic pattern of dominance and control, or what some researchers have called "patriarchal terrorism."[51] If you see signs of this in your relationship, leaving will be a risk—but we believe these signs also give you strong reason to leave.

REPORTING AND PROTECTION ORDERS

So if these are the risk factors, what are you to do about them? One of the practical precautions you can take is to report the abuse, and file a protection order. These are frightening words—we know. But we will walk you through what you need to do.

First of all, domestic violence is one of the most chronically un-derreported crimes—which limits what can be done about it.[52] Only about one-quarter of all physical assaults, one-fifth of all rapes, and one-half of all stalking incidents perpetuated against females by inti-mate partners are reported to the police.[53]

Why isn't it reported? These facts suggest that most victims of intimate partner violence do not consider the justice system an appro-priate vehicle for resolving conflicts with intimates.

Unfortunately, some have good reason to distrust the justice system. According to a study based on the National Violence Against Women Survey, for example, approximately 20% of victims annually obtain civil protection orders against former partners. But about one-half of those orders against intimate partners who physically assaulted them were violated.

But the police can be an effective deterrent. Steven Tracy points out that a 1986 Bureau of Justice Statistics survey concluded that women who reported their abuse to authorities were far less likely to be assaulted again than the wives who submitted to the abuse and did not contact the authorities.[54] Specifically, the survey found that 41% of wives who did not report their abusive husbands to the police were attacked again within six months, whereas only 15% of abused wives who reported the abuse to authorities were assaulted again.[55]

The bottom line? The justice system may not be an absolute guar-antee, but if you are honest and up front about the danger your abuser poses, the police can be a key to safety. If you take that first step, re-member that there are resources that the police can offer you—people to talk to and make plans with you—that can make all the other steps easier. They've done it before—you are not alone.

THE POWER OF NAMING VIOLENCE FOR WHAT IT IS

Naming and describing the evil done to you does not ensure au-tomatic personal healing. However, it does provide clarity, which may motivate your path to safety. On the other hand, if domestic violence is not defined, named, or described, then it remains hidden.

In the Bible, the psalmist never shies away from telling the truth of his dire circumstances—and neither should you. By naming injustice, violence, and lies, you acknowledge to God—and to yourself— that things are not the way they are meant to be. That very longing for wrongs to be righted speaks to your dignity, value, and worth as one created by God.

Acknowledging the trauma you have experienced is vital to your healing, but it is only the first step. As you begin to come to terms with your abuse, further healing will come as you are able to interpret the effect of what happened to you within a larger pattern of meaning. The first step toward doing this is to look closely at the effects of domestic violence and the accompanying emotions.

5

What Are the Effects
of Domestic Violence?

In the moment, it's hard to see how deeply domestic violence can affect you. Internal trauma is not only *done to you* but also *experienced by you*, the victim. These internal—and deeply personal—places of a victim's heart, will, and emotions need an equally personal application of the grace of God. If this is you, please turn to chapter 6.

While the statistics shows us the staggering prevalence of abuse today, what is even more staggering is to think about the damage done to each and every victim as an individual. Abusers often find ways to hurt the whole person. They shred their victim's sense of self-worth, crush their wills, and violate their bodies. The effects are widespread and catastrophic—including physical, social, emotional, psychological, and spiritual damage. If left untended, these effects will be ongoing, no matter how long ago the abuse happened. This is why it is important to deal with them honestly now.

Being abused is the very opposite of what God intends for you. In stark contrast to the effects of abuse, God wants you to be physically, socially, emotionally, psychologically, and spiritually whole. This is no abstract desire, either—this is something He actually enacts in your life by His grace.

So how does a person move from the effects of abuse into the effects of grace? That's what this chapter is here to help guide you through.

THE NEUROLOGICAL EFFECTS OF DOMESTIC VIOLENCE

Because abuse is harm done to the whole person, its whole person comprehensively feels its effects. And it all starts with the brain.

As neuroscientists discover more and more about how the brain works, they are also discovering the deep and lasting ways trauma impacts the brain. Trauma affects the brain in a way completely different from any other normal memories—which is vitally important in empowering those who have experienced abuse to know that they are not going crazy. Rather, the trauma gets "stuck" in the wrong part of the brain. In this part of the brain, trauma is misperceived as ongoing rather than part of the past. Because the trauma is experienced as a current event, it infuses and continues to play itself out in all areas of an individual's life: her emotional well-being, her physical health, her relationships, her faith, her overall functionality. Until it is moved into the right part of the brain (the frontal cortex), there will be ongoing physical and neurological problems.

In a very real sense, traumatic memory does not know time. That's why the platitude "Time heals all wounds" is very unhelpful.

It is appropriate to call domestic violence traumatic. "Trauma" is understood as a state of being negatively overwhelmed. It is the experience of terror, loss of control, of helplessness during a stressful event that threatens one's physical and/or psychological well-being. In her study of traumatic injuries, professor Jennifer Beste writes: "The especially sinister side of trauma is that, even when the event has ended, it has only begun to shatter one's key assumptions about one's self and one's relation to others in the world."[1] Indeed, after the trauma of domestic violence is long over, many victims experience intense emotional distress and frequent flashbacks of the abuse as they struggle emotionally and cognitively to adjust their sense of reality.

In addition to misplaced trauma in the brain, domestic abuse also triggers dramatic chemical changes in the brain. Studies show that living in a constant state of anxiety and anticipation of the next emergency can cause significant neurochemical and structural changes in the brain.[2] These changes can result in impaired cognition, psychiatric disorders, neuronal cell death, and even reduction in the size of the brain structure.[3, 4]

Because domestic violence is traumatizing, women who have survived domestic violence are significantly more likely to develop mental disorders, dysfunction, and disability than non-abused women.[5] These may include anxiety, depression, eating disorders, self-mutilation, substance abuse, post-traumatic stress disorder (PTSD), and suicide attempts.[6] Sadly, research of women with a history of suicide attempts indicates that up to 50% of them have experienced intimate violence.[7] Additionally, as many as 66% of female inpatients with mental illness have been abused.[8] Overall, there is a pattern of social disadvantage, disability, and impaired quality of life among women who have experienced domestic violence.

All of this stands as another indicator that you—and your brain— have been designed for health wholeness. You were made for more than this. Your brain, body, and soul were never intended to be subjected to such a traumatic toll.

While some victims eventually experience a gradual decrease in the intensity of emotions and memories surrounding the abuse, others re-experience the traumatic memories as though the original abuse were presently occurring. Subsequently, they develop a host of responses now identified as post-traumatic stress disorder (PTSD) symptoms, which is usually associated with combat war veterans. Most victims of domestic violence experience some kind of post-traumatic distress.[9] And in fact, victims of domestic violence are at least twice as likely to suffer from PTSD than non-abused women.

One of the most important things to know about the impact of abuse is that these mood swings and dysfunctions are a natural and normal way of dealing with trauma. Unfortunately, many people look at these symptoms and think that the problem lies with the victim, when in fact these responses to trauma are perfectly normal. If you are sensing these effects in your life, you are not "going mad." You are not doing anything wrong. You are processing an extreme situation, in very normal and expected ways. And to friends and family of victims of abuse, we would encourage you to give her all the support and grace you can while she processes through this trauma and its effects.

THE EMOTIONAL EFFECTS OF DOMESTIC VIOLENCE

Of course, neurological effects happen where we do not see or usually recognize them. But the emotional effects of domestic abuse are often intensely felt and painfully realized.

Ann Jones and Susan Schecter, who campaigned internationally against violence against women, identified five key feelings experienced by women across the map who were abused by their partners: "fear, shame, guilt, anger, and the nameless feeling of 'going crazy.'" [10]

Of course there are many more. Embarrassment, degradation, denial, a profound sense of emptiness, guilt, a sense of powerlessness, anger, a sense of helplessness, vulnerability, fear, depression, isolation, exhaustion, and/or anxiety. The emotional aftermath of abuse has a wide range, but all of these feelings are normal for someone going through domestic violence. [11] And they are all common effects of having one's desire—an intense desire, and rightfully so—for relief, protection, hope, justice, and vindication cut short.

Still, just because these emotions are typical does not make them less painful. Beyond the initial confusion, apathy, and despair felt by a victim of domestic violence, there is a continuing loss of confidence, energies, and initiative. These emotional wounds of the violent situation can be debilitating. They can be so paralyzing that sometimes she is unable to cope and make decisions that are sometimes necessary when leaving a violent situation. [12] A woman suffering from such side effects may have the desire to escape the violence but may simply be unable on her own to make her desires a reality.

In addition to finding the energies to take necessary action to protect and preserve herself, the victim will also need to know where to find assistance. For a victim who has not even been allowed a say in the running of her own home, finding this help can be an overwhelming prospect. Unless a victim knows where to find help, she is unlikely to leave. If this sounds like your situation or the situation of someone you know, we have made some suggestions in appendix 2 for those who need guidance in getting started.

THE PHYSICAL EFFECTS OF DOMESTIC VIOLENCE

Surgeon General C. Everett Koop reported that domestic violence is the greatest single cause of injury to American women.[13] Domestic violence is the leading cause of injury to women between the ages of 15 and 44 in the United States, more than car accidents, muggings, and rapes combined.[14] And yet less than one-fifth of victims reporting an injury from intimate partner violence sought medical treatment following the injury.[15]

Stalking and physical injury are also widely connected, and this is happening more than some might think. One in 12 women have been stalked in their lifetime,[16] and two-thirds of those women were stalked by a current or former intimate partner.[17] But it doesn't usually end with just stalking. Over 81% of women stalked by a current or former intimate partner are also physically assaulted by that partner, and 31% are also sexually assaulted by that partner.[18]

And in the worst-case scenario, their stalkers seek murder. Women are killed by intimate partners—husbands, lovers, ex-husbands, or ex-lovers—more often than by any other category of killer.[19] The U.S. Department of Justice and F.B.I. report that approximately one-third of murdered women are killed by an intimate partner.[20] It is the leading cause of death for African-American women aged 15 to 45 and the seventh leading cause of premature death for U.S. women overall.[21] Intimate partner homicides make up 40–50 percent of all murders of women in the United States.[22] Nationwide, an average of three women are killed by a current or former intimate partner every day.[23]

In 70–80% of intimate partner homicides, no matter which partner was killed, the man physically abused the woman before the murder.[24] One of the primary ways, then, to decrease intimate partner homicide is to identify and intervene promptly when it is discovered that a woman is being abused.

As one researcher states, "A woman is hit an average of 35 times before she calls the police, and she will leave her abuser five or six times before she leaves for good."[25] Additionally, sexual assault occurs in approximately 45% of abusive relationships.[26] These are all serious offenses to be reported and signal a clear alarm that intervention is necessary to escape this cycle of abuse.

But even apart from these realities of stalking, injury, and death, domestic violence affects victims in other physical ways. Because our bodies are so intricately connected with our minds, the emotional toll of domestic violence often plays out in one's physical health.

Women who have experienced violence by an intimate partner are more likely than women who have not to experience all of the following: asthma, diabetes, irritable bowel syndrome, gastrointestinal disorders, substance abuse, sexually transmitted diseases, gynecological or pregnancy complications, depression, anxiety, low self-esteem, suicide attempts, frequent headaches, chronic pain, difficulty with sleeping, activity limitations, poor physical health, and poor mental health. These consequences can lead to hospitalization, disability, and in some cases, death.[27]

The involuntary physical effects of domestic abuse fill a wide range, from headaches and muscle tension to choking sensations, vomiting, and panic attacks. Victims of domestic abuse also at times use coping mechanisms that are self-harming, such as developing cutting, substance abuse, eating disorders, or suicide.

THE SPIRITUAL EFFECTS OF DOMESTIC VIOLENCE

If such is the dramatic effects of abuse on a woman's brain, body, and emotions, what is the impact on her spiritual journey? As many abused Christian women have stated, it is a profound one.

Not only have their bodies been harmed, but their emotions have been damaged, their relationships have been put in peril, and their spirits have been crushed.[28] The abused woman is constantly faced with her abuser's forced and false reality that she is worthless—though God has created her with unspeakable worth. Her abuser's perception of her works at a complete crosscurrent with God's perception of her, and as a result, she often cannot determine which is real.

Feminist writer Carol Adams explains and summarizes what domestic violence victims have lost:[29]

- Safety and normalcy and peace of mind that accompanies one's sense of safety.
- The ability to set boundaries and have them and her privacy respected.
- Her sense of reality as it is duplicated by the abuser's sense of reality, her sense of direction as the abuser's control overwhelms it, her sense of decency and her belief in decency as it gives way to violation and being violable.
- Her self-esteem, ability to trust, confidence in herself, sense that the world is just and that God is just.
- The increasing sense of interpersonal resources.
- Feelings such as faith, hope, charity, worth, innocence, goodness, joy, love, connectedness, intimacy, and purity are all seriously undermined.

As any woman who has experienced domestic violence knows, abuse affects the whole person. However, so does grace. And grace is a powerful catalyst for healing.

We like to look at healing from abuse through the lens of grace because we've seen so many victims who identify with disgrace. But to move from one to the other, we need to take a closer look at the emotions behind this feeling of disgrace.

First of all, we need to determine what emotions are and what emotions are not.

Emotions are based on cognitive assessment and belief; they are not simply experienced. An emotion is not an impression—a feeling or a unique sort of internal experience that just happens to a person and then is named and described.[30] Neither are emotions merely physiological impulses that can be simply ignored, trivialized, or controlled.[31] No, emotions are a sort of barometer for how we view ourselves, our personal experiences, and our relationships with others. Human emotions are often cast as either "good" or "bad." The reality is, they can be either. Our emotions can aid us in better understanding who we believe ourselves to be and who we believe God to be. As Dan Allender and Tremper Longman say in their book *The Cry of the Soul*, "every emotion, though horizontally provoked, nevertheless reflects something about the vertical dimension: our relationship with God."[32]

Therefore, if we listen to them, we have much to learn.

What this means for victims of domestic violence is that your emotions are important and valid. They are not just chemicals in your brain and physiological responses to stimuli. Your emotions are to be taken seriously and listened to. They are powerful revealers of what you believe about God, yourself, your experience of abuse, others, and the world. And when you better understand these emotions, you are better able to take control of and shape them according to what is most beneficial for you. This emotional understanding can help you on the journey from disgrace to boundless grace.

NEW EMOTIONS

Emotion, as we've discussed, is linked to beliefs. Because abuse encourages you to adopt false beliefs—"I am worthless," or "I've done something wrong and deserve to be punished"—you can also develop dysfunctional emotions such as shame and distress. The good news is that reorienting your beliefs can also gradually help your emotions return to normal. Our hope is that the grace of God—which declares you valuable, beautiful, and worthy of respect—would be key to dismantling the debilitating emotions caused by your abuse and nurturing new, positive emotions within you.

This is not an act of denial, in which you pretend to take on happy emotions but a deliberate exercise in personal transformation. The late

Paul Holmer, a philosopher at Yale, explains: "Part of the whole sense-making that Christianity provides is a whole panoply of new emotion. Hope, fear of the Lord, contrition about oneself, love—these and more are not just variations of the familiar or permutations of something we already have, they are new affects, new forms of pathos."[33]

And for such a transformation as this, we need a guide—which we find in the person of Jesus. We need to look to the gospel in order to investigate the new emotions that God offers to victims and how they relate to the current emotions that victims experience.

Too many people want to separate emotion from a theology of faith and suffering. Yet we believe the two must go together. Part of the reason we decided to write a book that combined emotion with theology is because we believe that Christianity has something powerful to offer to those who are in the midst of emotional turmoil. We wish to integrate suffering, faith, emotions, and theology. As theologian Don Saliers writes: "Whatever else it may include, the Christian faith is a pattern of deep emotions."[34]

When those deep emotions are emotions of suffering, however, it can be difficult to see clearly. This is where grace offers an incredible gift—the gift of refuting faulty thinking and replacing it with God-given truth. What God's grace can offer you is simply this: it will show you who you are, undistorted. And it will point you to the God who loves and comforts those in need.

This is an important point to highlight. We are all powerless to heal ourselves. We cannot simply "snap out of it." We need an intervention. That intervention, we believe, is called grace.

What you need are not self-produced positive statements but God's statements about His response to your pain. How can you be rid of these dysfunctional emotions and their effects? How can you be rid of your disgrace? We believe that God's grace to you acts in two ways. First, by showing you who you are in relation to Him, He dismantles the beliefs that give power to disgrace. But more than that, grace re-creates what violence has destroyed.

To understand how this grace works on a practical level, consider this passage from Westminster Theological Seminary professor Carl Trueman, "Others might tell me that I am a failure, an idiot, a clown, evil, incompetent, vicious, dangerous, pathetic, etc., and these words are not just descriptive: they have a certain power to make me these things, in the eyes of others and even in my own eyes." In the case of domestic abuse, maybe the problem is also actions. You have had things done to you that have left their mark. You can't get away from the memory of those things; you feel, deep inside, as though what the abuser has said to you or done to you show you to be bad or worthless, and you can't break that image.

However, God has the last word—and His word is the one that counts. Martin Luther wrote that salvation in the Christian sense means that God makes an entirely new creature out of the messy raw material that He begins with. He does this in the same way He created the heavens and the earth—by saying so: "God calls into existence things which do not exist. He does not speak grammatical words; He speaks true and existent realities . . . when He says: 'Sun, shine,' the sun is there at once and shines."

On this, Trueman notes: "But . . . God speaks louder, and his Word is more powerful. You may call me a liar, and you speak truth, for I have lied; but if God declares me righteous, then my lies and your insult are not the final word, nor the most powerful word. Only as God speaks his Word to me, and as I hear that Word in faith, is my reality transformed, and . . . the insults of others, of my own sinful nature, and of the evil one himself cease to constitute my reality."[35]

This means that when Christians talk about God declaring us "righteous," or "good," because of Christ, that new identity is the one that takes hold in our lives—even if we don't feel good or righteous. When we turn to God, the new identity begins to take deeper and deeper hold. Old habits and beliefs about ourselves begin to fall away—and with them, the torn-up, dysfunctional emotions that accompany abuse likewise fall behind.

Part 2

WOMEN, DOMESTIC VIOLENCE, AND THE BIBLE

6

Does the Grace of God Apply to Me?[1]

There is an epidemic of abuse, and victims need the kind of hope and help that only the gospel of Jesus Christ can provide.

Many victims feel that God is punishing them, and they look for causes in themselves. They may think, "I haven't been a good wife or mother, so God is punishing me," or "I did something wrong when I was a teenager, so God is punishing me," or "I haven't been a good enough Christian, so God is punishing me."

None of these are true. For God is a God of grace, not of karma. Karma says you get what you deserve. Grace says the opposite. Grace is getting what you don't deserve and not getting what you do deserve. It's the most important concept in the Bible, in Christianity, and—we believe—in the world. A shorthand way of thinking about grace is "mercy, not merit." God is not interested in punishing you or making you pay. He's interested in lavishing you with His grace.

This kind of unconditional love is a difficult concept to wrap your mind around. Many of us think—whether we admit it or not—there must be some breaking point where God gives up on us. This is so common for all of us, and particularly for victims. After all, if your partner has made a habit of reaching his limit of love for you, this shapes your understanding of relationships. In this chapter we want to connect the dots between the life, death, and resurrection of Jesus[2] and the disgrace of domestic violence. The deepest message of the ministry of Jesus and of the entire Bible is the grace of God to sinners and sufferers. Grace is the love of God shown to the unlovely; the peace of God given to the restless; the unmerited favor of God. Grace is love that cares and stoops and rescues.[3] Grace is unconditional love toward a person who does not deserve it.[4]

Grace is "one-way love," and it is directed at you.[5] This is the opposite of your experience, which is one-way violence. It seeks you out even if you do not deal out any violence in return.

Grace, on the other hand, is being loved when you are or feel unlovable. Grace has the power to turn despair into hope. Grace listens, lifts up, cures, transforms, and heals. To the experience of one-way violence, God brings one-way love.

One-way love does not avoid you but comes near, not because of personal merit but because of your need. It is the lasting transformation that takes place in human experience, able to change your experience with pain, suffering, and brokenness.

Disgrace is the opposite of grace and is experienced by the numerous victims of domestic violence. This experience of feeling disgrace has nothing to do with what you have done but because something disgraceful was done to you. You didn't cause yourself disgrace—someone else did, and it was wrong. The disgrace that results from domestic violence has a way of grinding victims down and heaping huge burdens on them. But God uses the gospel of grace to eliminate that disgrace and heal its effects.

Hurting people need something from the outside to stop the downward spiral. Fortunately, grace floods in from the outside at the point when hope to change oneself is lost.

God, in His grace, declares that you will be healed of your disgrace. Contrary to the proponents of the healing benefits of self-esteem for victims, this promise does not come from within you but from outside of you. One-way love does not command, "Heal thyself!" but declares "You will be healed!" Take a look at this promise in Jeremiah 17:14, "Heal me, Lord, and I will be healed; save me and I will be saved, for you are the one I praise."

God's one-way love replaces your need to save yourself and is the true path to healing. In His eyes, you are already worthwhile. This is astonishingly good news, and it highlights the contrast between disgrace and grace or one-way violence and one-way love.

You don't need to heal your own wounds—God will do that. But what you can do is cling to the promise that God is strong when you are weak, and that He is close to the brokenhearted. Allow God to fulfill His promises to you, after so many promises have been broken.

Even if you have been wounded by one-way violence, please know this: your story does not end with abuse. Your life was intended for more than denial, identity crisis, shame, anger, and despair. The abuse does not define you or have the last word on your identity. Yes, it is part of the story, but it is not the end of the story. Let's take a look at how this one-way grace transforms even our darkest disgrace.

Some of the most prevalent responses to domestic violence include denial, distorted self-image, shame, guilt, anger, and despair. Let's look at each one and see how God applies grace to disgrace through the gospel of Jesus.

DENIAL

Denial and minimization are key methods victims use, as a means of lessening or coping with the trauma from domestic violence.

Initially, denial can slow the process down to create a buffer or safety zone so survivors can ease into coping with difficult emotions. Prolonged denial, however, may backfire by increasing the pain in the long run. For if a victim cannot come to terms with the severe mental and emotional tolls she has sustained, she cannot truly heal from it.

What's more, God never minimizes the pain you have suffered. Instead of denying what has happened to you, He mourns over it. He identifies with you through Jesus' pain on the cross, and He has compassion. Jesus, too, "was despised and rejected by mankind, a man of suffering, and familiar with pain" (Isa. 53:3). Another version says He was "acquainted with grief." This is a God who not only suffered for His people but also suffers with them. Jesus knows what it means to be alone, naked, bleeding, and crying out to God. He shared in absolute abandonment and the pain of sufferers, and was a victim of violence and suffered injustice. While the cross shows us that God understands pain and does not judge you for your feelings of grief, the resurrection shows you that God is active in restoring peace—that He conquered sin and is reversing its effects.

God knows your suffering. Rather than denying it, He grieves with you. You are not encouraged to be silent or deny but to feel and express your emotions, to cry or weep, to grieve the destruction you experienced. Because of Jesus, you have the privilege to confidently go to God and receive grace and mercy.

IDENTITY

Domestic violence victims fight the constant struggle to maintain their identity when the abuser is distorting it. This kind of disgrace slowly erodes a victim's self-image. A negative self-image, provoked by an abuser, fuels an identity founded on self-condemnation.

Domestic violence maligns a victim's sense of self and communicates that they are stupid, filthy, foolish, worthless, defiled, impure, damaged, gross, screwed-up, unwanted, or dirty.

But God never calls you any of these things. And this is not the identity He has given you.

Making the transition from a victim identity to an identity in Christ is offered in God's redemptive work through Jesus. Of course, if you are a victim of domestic violence, then that is a part of your story that you should not deny or minimize. But if you let it become *the* reigning story about you, then your identity will be founded on disgrace. God offers the redemptive story told in Scripture to you, and you may claim it as your story at any time. The identity from that story is founded on grace in at least two specific ways.

Firstly, if you have faith in Christ, God calls you certain things that convey value. The "people of God" is one of the most significant. This intimacy of God's concern for His people is seen clearly in the declaration that you are a child of God if you trust in Christ (1 John 3:1–2). This is, perhaps, the most remarkable thing you can be called. This new identity is rooted in being adopted into God's family. God adopted you and accepted you because He loves you. You didn't do anything to deserve His love, and yet He loves you unconditionally.

Secondly, because of faith in Christ, you receive the righteousness or the goodness of God. The strength, wisdom, humility, courage, and generous love that define God slowly begin to define who you are instead of your past.

We find in 2 Corinthians 5:21 an identity-altering statement: "God made him who had no sin to be sin for us, so that in him we might become the righteousness of God." This passage tells us that God isn't saving good people but damaged people. And we are all damaged because we all live in a fallen, broken world. He takes that damage on Himself, and in an incredible exchange, He looks at us and sees only His own righteousness. He tells us that this is our identity even when it doesn't feel as though it is—even when we seem stuck in the things we've done and had done to us—and helps us grow into it. Theologians call this imputation, which is ascribing characteristics to someone that they do not have by nature. Imputation is the crediting in our favor, from the standpoint of God, who is the source of all judgment, the perfect moral worth of Jesus. It also implies the humility of Jesus, who took on our full burden of disgraces so that He could make this astounding transfer.

By faith, we are in Christ and as such we are seen as He is. His righteousness, holiness, and blamelessness are imputed to us. This dramatically transforms our identity.

Instead of damaged, broken, filthy, useless, failure, or sinful, God uses new words to lavishly redefine those who are His: redeemed and forgiven (Eph. 1:6–8), made righteous (Rom. 5:1), new creation (2 Cor. 5:17), God's workmanship (Eph. 2:10), reconciled to God (2 Cor. 5:18), saint (1 Cor. 1:2; Eph. 1:1; Phil. 1:1), chosen, holy, and beloved (Col. 3:12), child of light, not darkness (1 Thess. 5:5), pure, blameless, glory of God (Phil. 1:10–11), holy, blameless, and above reproach (Col. 1:21–22), and the righteousness of God (2 Cor. 5:21). "I will call them 'my people' who are not my people," God tell us, "and I will call her 'my loved one' who is not my loved one" (Rom. 9:25). If you believe in Christ, your identity is deeper than any of your wounds. Your new identity is more secure and stable than any other identity that has been attributed to you. That means you are not doomed to live as a victim. It doesn't eliminate your wounds nor silence your cry for deliverance or healing. But it does mean those wounds are not the final word on who you are. They don't enslave you and determine your life.

As we will see in Part 3 of this book as we venture into the Psalms, it's perfectly natural to ask, "If I belong to God, why am I suffering like this?" These questions are more than okay. In order to have the cycle of disgrace broken, we need a God before whom we can put aside the disguises. What we're saying for right now is to trust that God hears you and won't reject you, and that when He looks at you, He doesn't see a "failure" or "damaged goods."

SHAME

Even if abuse is not your fault—and it is never your fault—shame can be a difficult emotion to fight. Jean-Paul Sartre, the French existentialist writer, accurately describes shame as "a hemorrhage of the soul": that is, a painful, unexpected, and disorienting experience. Shame has the power to take our breath away and smother us with condemnation, rejection, and disgust. To be shamed is to be abased and dishonored, to be rejected from the community—especially when a victim is not believed or supported, told to be silent, or blamed.

Shame is a painfully confusing experience—a sort of mental and emotional disintegration that makes us acutely aware of our inadequacies, shortcomings, and is often associated with a shrinking feeling of failure. It can be particularly destructive if a victim feels stigmatized by withering, energy-draining feelings of worthlessness. Often victims will attempt to numb this pain through drugs, alcohol, sex, power, success, or whatever else enables them to stop feeling.

We should be clear that we're not suggesting that you deal with shame by becoming "more religious." Whatever your current faith involvement is, trying to make up for shame with more religious activities will only short-circuit your healing process and make you feel worse. But we do believe in a God who deliberately became acquainted with shame, and because of this, He is well placed to deal with us in our own shame.

Jesus was well acquainted with this emotion. Throughout His adult life, He actively pursued the company of outcasts who were considered damaged and unfit for normal society. They were considered "unclean"—morally, socially, or religiously. His solidarity with the shamed and excluded of His day led to being shamed Himself. The Romans used crosses to humiliate the criminals they considered especially despicable.

So whatever shame you are experiencing in your life right now, please know that Jesus is no stranger to this ugly emotion. He's not at all put off by whatever deep, dark secret that is causing us to feel crushed; in fact, He is interested in reaching right into the middle of it and changing it. What's more, the domestic violence you experienced was not your fault—not at all. This realization all by itself can bring great freedom and relief from shame.

ANGER

Domestic violence is unquestionably an evil, sinful act that understandably elicits anger. The Bible condemns domestic violence and God hates it (more on this in chapter 8). Deep in the hearts of victims, anger swells up against the perpetrator, their rage inflamed by suffering. Anger is a natural and even healthy response to domestic violence. While nearly all victims appropriately experience anger, most express it poorly or not at all.

It is likely that you have been discouraged from expressing your anger. Most victims feel pressure from their families, society, or religion to ignore or suppress it. But suppression does not help anger to dissipate over time. Instead, it will turn into bitterness, hatred, and revengeful obsessions. In fact, unresolved or denied anger can become a destructive force in your life. Anger holds you hostage and leaves you vindictive, addicted, embittered, immoral, and unbelieving.

It is important to note that Scripture does not always describe anger as sin. God is angrier over the sin committed against you even more than you are. He is angry because what happened to you was evil and it harmed you. Certainly Scripture is clear that anger is a dangerous emotion, though it can be righteous (directed at sin) or it can be sinful (delighting in vindication). God is the only one who can remain perfect in His anger and never sin in His anger. But we can exhibit godly anger by participating in God's anger against injustice and sin. In this sense, you are not only *invited* to be angry at evil, you are *expected* to be angry. You are invited by God to cry out for Him to do what He has promised to do: destroy evil and remove everything that harms others and defames God's name.

Because vengeance is God's, you are free from the exhausting hamster wheel of vindictive behavior. Victims can trust God to make all wrongs right so they can get on with their lives and not fixate on bitterness and hatred. God's wrath is a source of positive hope for the victim. You know that God loves you and will destroy the evil that has harmed you. Because vengeance is God's, you don't have to be vengeful; you can love and forgive your enemy.

Receiving forgiveness and love from God through Christ is essential to understanding forgiveness. Because God forgave you for your sins, you are now free to forgive others. Jesus received God's anger and punishment so those guilty of cosmic treason would be forgiven. As sinners who have received mercy instead of wrath, we have the otherwise inexplicable capability simultaneously to hate wrong and to give love to those who do wrong. What God did for us becomes the power to change. God's one-way love toward us amid our sin undermines our bitterness and can prompt forgiveness of those who sin against us.

It is important to be clear on this topic because abusers may cite Scripture to insist that their victims forgive them. A victim may then feel guilty if she cannot do so. Forgiveness, however, does not mean forgetting the abuse or pretending that it did not happen. Neither is possible, because sin has consequences and forgiveness does not remove those consequences. Forgiveness is *not* permission to repeat the abuse. Nor does it require restoring the relationship. As a matter of fact, it may be dangerous and life-threatening to restore the relationship. Rather, forgiveness means that the victim decides to let go of the experience in order for God to deal justly with her abuser. It is the decision to move on and refuse to tolerate abuse of any kind again.

DESPAIR

If left unaddressed, identity issues, shame, and anger may all compound in feelings of despair—a commonly reported symptom of domestic violence. Feeling that you lost something—whether it's your innocence, youth, health, trust, confidence, or sense of safety—can lead to despair. For those who have experienced the evil of domestic violence, it's likely that you've had an encounter with despair and depression.

Depression adds seemingly inescapable weight to the existential experience of despair. For some victims, feelings of hopelessness and helplessness come and go, while for others these feelings seem inescapable every day. When the feelings of powerlessness are internalized, self-hatred and self-pity intensify to the point of despair. Despair deadens our hearts to the hope that we will be rescued, redeemed, and relived of suffering.

But there is hope. Rather than being simply a desire for a particular outcome that is uncertain, hope is characterized by certainty in the Bible. Hope is sure because God is behind the promise, and the hope you need right now borrows from God's faithfulness in the past and anticipation of His faithfulness in the future. The basis you have for hope is the resurrection of Jesus from the dead.

Of course, looking to Jesus' resurrection is a spiritual truth that is powerful to lift you out of your despair. But sometimes you will need practical help as well. In addition to this great spiritual hope, we also are blessed to live in a time when we can seek medical and psychiatric help. All of us need the eternal hope of the gospel, but for some of us, we may need to consider the efficacy of prescription medication, or meeting with a psychiatric professional as well.

If you need medical treatment or professional help for your depression, it is our hope that you will seek it. But either way, the truth of Jesus' resurrection stands true for you as well.

Because Jesus conquered death through the resurrection, death and evil done to you is not the end of your story. Because of Jesus' resurrection, you also can have hope. In being united to Christ, you too will conquer as you look through the eyes of faith to the one who has accomplished everything on your behalf through His death and resurrection.

The resurrection of Jesus has also launched new creation and the coming of a new heavens and new earth where disgrace will be replaced by grace, anxiety will give way to peace, and despair will be banished. In the new creation God will be with us; He will bring peace and we will be perfected. Jesus is the first of that new creation. He has already given you new birth into that new creation and promises to complete it in you, making you gloriously, perfectly like Him. What about now? God has not only given us a sure hope but sent the person of His Holy Spirit to comfort us in the despair and isolation we face in the present.

Godly despair is the groan of the Holy Spirit, and while you may see no explanation for your pain, He knows there is an answer and lovingly communicates your pain to a sovereign God who listens. Your God is strong and He—not the evil done to you—will have the final say about you. That hope animates groans within ourselves (Rom. 8:23) that everything will someday be renewed. We will be delivered from all sin and misery. Every tear will be wiped away when evil is no more.

So we groan in pain because the pain is still painful. But we also groan in hope because we know what is to come. Hope is a positive expectation for something in the future as opposed to despair that sees only pain and hardship. Biblically, hope has the power to encourage in the present because it is based on sure future expectations. As French philosopher Gabriel Marcel wrote, "Hope is a memory of the future." This side of glory, we will not be fully redeemed and satisfied. But sorrow opens the heart to the desire for the hope of redemption to be fully realized.

WHAT GRACE HAS TO SAY TO YOU

Domestic violence is uniquely devastating precisely because it distorts the foundational realities of what it means to be human—the realities of our relationships. As we look to Scripture, we find domestic violence perverts relationships to a place where they are so far removed from the true way God intended relationships to be—filled with peace, love, and mutual serving. Yet domestic violence creates in the victim's mind a tragic and perverse linkage between love, intimacy, sex, and shame that was never meant to be.

This is where grace has something to say. Trusting Jesus isn't a faint hope in generic spiritual sentiments but is banking our hope and future on the real historical Jesus who lived, died, and rose from the dead. Grace is available because Jesus went through the valley of the shadow of death and rose from death. Jesus responds to victims' pain and past. The gospel engages our life with all its pain, shame, rejection, lostness or bewilderment, sin, and death.

So now, to your pain, the gospel says, "You will be healed." To your shame, the gospel says, "You can now come to God in confidence." To your rejection, the gospel says, "You are accepted!" To your lostness, the gospel says, "You are found and I won't ever let you go." To your sin, the gospel says, "You are forgiven and God declares you pure and righteous." To your death, the gospel says, "You were dead, but now you are alive." The message of the gospel redeems what has been destroyed and applies grace to disgrace.

What Does the Bible Say about Women?

Most incidents of domestic abuse can be traced back to a single, toxic assumption: that women are inherently inferior to men.

Yet this is an idea the Bible soundly refutes. From the beginning in Genesis, Scripture teaches that women and men are equal and created in God's image. This is repeated and expanded on through the entire Old Testament. Additionally, Jesus Himself always respected and promoted the human dignity of women, which sets the tone for how the New Testament writers and early church viewed women.

However, we recognize that some may believe that the biblical view of women can be controversial due to its apparent patriarchal social norms. Some abusers—as well as victims—may believe that the Bible views and instructs treatment of women as marginalized, second-class citizens. Further, some claim the Bible upholds a masculine religion rooted in a male God. Still others claim the New Testament—or our human misinterpretation of it—denigrates women and curtails their active involvement in the church by keeping them subservient to men.

These are all serious accusations. And in this chapter, we'll consider each of them more closely. Contrary to what some may believe, however, the Scriptures actually paint a very favorable picture of women, where women are equally created in the image of God and highly valued by Him. The first word on women in the Bible serves functionally as the last word on the subject: women are created in the image of God and are highly valued by Him.

Let's take a look at what the Bible has to say about women in the

Old Testament, the New Testament, how Jesus views women, and women in the church.

MADE IN GOD'S IMAGE

Both men and woman are created in God's image, and as a result, they are both of inherent value. Genesis 1:26–27 reads, "Let us make man in our image. So God created man in his own image, in the image of God he created him; male and female he created them" (ESV).

The creation account emphasizes that men and women are made in God's image and begins with this description rather than focusing on their sex. As one scholar remarks, "It is significant that the man and woman are not first defined by their sexuality or gender; they are first defined by the fact that together they are created in the image of God."[1]

Being made in God's image, you are not a second-class citizen. Furthermore, as theologian Wayne Grudem notes, this first male-female relationship was created to reflect the unconditional, mutual love within the Trinity. He explains, "Just as there was fellowship and communication and sharing of glory among the members of the Trinity before the world was made … so God made Adam and Eve in such a way that they would share love and communication and mutual giving of honor to one another in their interpersonal relationship."[2]

As early as Genesis, we see God's design for human relationships: they are intended for mutual love, not coercion or control over the other.

Additionally, God shows no preference in who He gives His likeness to reflect. As Grudem notes, both men and women are given the moral, spiritual, mental, relational, and physical qualities that reflect God. All of these apply equally to male and female.

This is repeated in Genesis 2:18: "The Lord God said, 'It is not good for the man to be alone. I will make a helper suitable for him.'" To help does not mean to serve, implying that God created women to serve men and suggesting they are inferior to them. Rather, the word "helper" (*ezer* in Hebrew) most often refers to God in the Old

Testament usage (1 Sam. 7:12; Ps. 121:1–2). Therefore, there is no suggestion at all of female inferiority.

The creation story sets the tone for men and women to be seen as equals. Our Lord doesn't want you to be abused for any reason, but least of all because of who you are.

WOMEN AND THE OLD TESTAMENT

An in-depth study of women in the Old Testament is beyond our scope, so this section will instead provide a sweeping overview, highlighting particularly important points. We'll begin by looking at the culture of the ancient Near East in comparison with Old Testament Judaism.

To understand women in the Old Testament, it's important to understand the historical and cultural context of the time period. In the ancient Near East the nuclear family was "closely tied in with other family units to form a clan or tribe," and the "senior male of the clan functioned in many cases as head of the whole and could be called upon to render judgment in cases involving even distant relations."[3] In these societies, the "husband's authority over his wife and family was a matter of civil law."[4] In ancient Assyrian culture (a little bit north of Israel), "laws continue the leadership of the family by the patriarch and reveal the role of women as property."[5]

As we have seen, the ancient Near East was overwhelmingly patriarchal. However, the God of the Bible often works *within* human contexts and cultures, rather than completely transforming them in one fell swoop. Consequently, while God did not change everything about ancient Near East culture that we moderns would like to see changed, His hand of mercy is still apparent within it.

With regard to specific biblical laws, scholar William Webb writes, "As one compares the biblical texts about women to their surrounding foreign context . . . a certain impression emerges. On the whole, the biblical material is headed toward an elevation of women in status and rights."[6]

One example, which may be helpful for this book, has to do with cases of rape—one of the most prominent acts of violence and abuse against women. In Old Testament law, "forcible rape is punishable by death and is explicitly linked to murder, a realization that rape is a crime of aggression and violence rather than sex, and that the girl is a victim (Deut. 22:25–27)."[7] Compare this to other neighboring cultures of the day, in which it was the woman who was punished.

Beyond elevated views of women in comparison to other cultural practices of the day, the Old Testament also offers many examples of the value of women. While women's roles did generally reflect the culture of their time, there are also striking examples of women who excelled in traditionally male roles. Consider the following examples:

- Deborah, who served as a judge—a leader of Israel (Judg. 4)
- Jael (Judg. 4)
- Miriam (Ex. 15:20–21)
- Huldah the prophetess (2 Kings 22:11–20)
- Woman of Tekoa (2 Sam. 14)
- Woman of Abel Beth Maacah (2 Sam. 20:14–22)
- Abigail, wife of wicked Nabal, who then married King David (1 Sam. 25)
- Queen Esther
- The woman of Proverbs 31, who performs duties beyond those of wife and mother

In addition to women leaders, we see God's special concern for women who may be socially disadvantaged. He institutes special care laws for widows (Deut. 10:18; Zech. 7:10), for example. He shows mercy to barren women for whom He provided children, such as Sarah and Rachel. And He demonstrates tenderness toward hurting women, such as Hannah in 1 Samuel 1; Hagar in Genesis 21:14–21; and Ruth and Naomi in the book of Ruth. Even within a male-dominated culture, we see the original intention of female dignity and worth shine through the stories and texts of the Old Testament.

Although critics point out that male-dominated imagery is found throughout the Old Testament in reference to God ("father," "warrior," or "jealous husband," for example), we also find feminine language and images applied to God. Some examples include the following:

- Seamstress (Gen. 3:21)
- Mother and nurse (Num. 11:12)
- Loving mother (Hos. 11:1, 3–4; Ps. 131:2)
- Motherly compassion (Jer. 31:20)
- God in birth pangs (Isa. 42:13–14)
- Israel in the womb of God the mother (Isa. 46:3–4)
- Nursing mother (Isa. 49:14–15)
- Comforting mother (Isa. 66:12–13)
- Midwife (Ps. 22:9)
- Wisdom personified as a woman (Prov.; Job 28)—in fact, many of the descriptions applied to Wisdom are also applied to Christ.

Of course, God being spirit is neither, strictly speaking, male or female in the embodied human sense. This sort of language is used in the Bible in order to better communicate to us in terms we can relate to. Nevertheless, it's important to point out that Old Testament descriptions of God encompass both the masculine and feminine.

JESUS AND WOMEN

Theologians have long said that to really know what God is like you should look to Jesus. Even Jesus claims that the way to know God is through Himself (John 14:6, 9). Employing that principle, we will next explore what God thinks about women by looking at how Jesus related to women.

Continuing the theme of the Old Testament, Jesus upheld the rights of women against accepted cultural conventions where they were often considered inferior to men. Jesus spoke with women (John 4), taught women (Luke 10:38–42), and included women as followers (Luke 8:2–3), even though this was socially objectionable.

Jesus featured women as characters in His parables, such as in the parable of the yeast (Matt. 13:33), the persistent widow (Luke 18:1–5), the 10 bridesmaids (Matt. 25:1–13), the poor widow's offering (Luke 21:1–4), and in His teachings on the end times (Matt. 24:19, 41). Women are also found throughout Jesus' ministry of miracles, healing, and forgiveness, including the account of the crippled woman (Luke 13:10–17), the woman who touched Jesus' garment (Matt. 9:20–22), the Gentile mother (Matt. 15:21–28), the daughter of Jairus (Matt. 9:18–26), women present at two resurrection accounts (Luke 7:11–17 and John 11), and in the compassion Jesus demonstrated toward shunned women (Luke 7:36–60; John 4; John 8:1–11). Underscoring the importance of women in the ministry of Jesus, they are the first to discover Jesus missing from His tomb. And after His resurrection, He appears first to women rather than to His male apostles (Matt. 28; Mark 16; Luke 24; John 20).

It is also telling that many of Jesus' followers were women, with several mentioned by name, including Mary, Martha, Joanna, Mary Magdalene, Susanna, Salome, and more. As New Testament scholar Dr. Craig Blomberg notes: "An unspecified number [of women] forms part of the larger company of disciples that regularly follows him [Jesus] on the road and forms His 'support team' (Luke 8:1–3; cf. Acts 1:14–15)."[8] Thus, as Blomberg's fellow New Testament scholar Ben Witherington comments, "Not only Jesus' teaching and actions, but also the relationships He was involved in and the events surrounding His death and burial, led to the acceptance of women as valid witnesses and genuine disciples of Jesus."[9]

Jesus also took scandalous stances on issues related to women. Witherington comments: "Jesus' rejection of divorce outright would have offended practically everyone of His day. [We should add here that we believe separation or divorce to be an option in abusive relationships.] Further, Jesus' view that the single state was a legitimate and

not abnormal calling for those to whom it was given, went against pre-
vailing views . . . It was this teaching which made it possible for women
also to assume roles other than those of wife and mother in Jesus' community." Witherington adds, "That Jesus did not endorse various ways
of making women 'scapegoats,' especially in sexual matters, placed Him
at odds with other rabbis, though doubtless even many Gentiles would
have thought that Jesus' rejection of the 'double standard' was taking
equality too far. Further, we do not find negative remarks about the
nature, abilities and religious potential of women in comparison to
men on the lips of Jesus . . ."[10]

Jesus also preserves and intensifies the "strong Old Testament em-
phasis on sexual propriety (Matt. 5:27–30; 19:1–12), but for the first
time makes clear that women and men will be judged by identical stan-
dards (Matt. 5:32; Mark 10:11–12). Luke frequently pairs episodes in
which men and women function in identical ways. Both Elizabeth and
Zechariah praise under the Spirit's inspiration (Luke 1:41–45, 67–79).
Both Simeon and Anna prophesy that in Christ they have seen Israel's
salvation (2:25–38). Male and female cripples receive identical healings (13:10–17; 14:1–6) . . . Clearly Luke wants to highlight God's
care for both genders and Jesus' concern to relate to both. The story
of Jesus meeting the Samaritan woman perhaps epitomizes his commitment to revolutionizing the lot of the disenfranchised of his day.
Despite strong cultural taboos against any social exchange between a
Jewish holy man and a sexually promiscuous Samaritan woman, Jesus
speaks to this woman in private, affirms her personhood and leads her
to faith in himself and to service as an evangelist (John 4:1–42)."[11]

Jesus also would have offended contemporary Jewish listeners
when in Matthew 5:27–28 He said, "You have heard that it was said,
'You shall not commit adultery.' But I say to you that everyone who
looks at a woman with lustful intent has already committed adultery with her in his heart" (ESV). New Testament professor Grant
Osborne says of the passage, "Jesus' teaching on lust in the antithesis
of [Matthew] 5:27–28 also exhibits two significant differences from

normal Jewish thought. First, Jesus places the blame squarely upon the man, whose own lustful look is the sin. Many rabbis blamed the woman, who according to them enticed the man. Second this obviously was not intended by Jesus to obviate contact with women. As already noted, Jesus often initiated such contacts and considered many women his friends. The problem of lust called for spiritual control on the man's part rather than the seclusion of women."[12]

But if Jesus was so affirming of women, why weren't any of His twelve apostles women? While all of the official twelve apostles were men, it's "not clear if this reflects any timeless principle besides a commitment to present the gospel to a given culture in ways which will most likely speed its acceptance."[13] As Roger Nicole writes, it does not "necessarily represent a discrimination, since the ministry of the apostles needed to be readily received and for that purpose the attitude of some of those to whom it would be addressed needed to be considered. Jesus used extensively the 'Father language' in his teaching, but once again this does not imply any contempt for motherhood. In its totality the attitude of our Lord was revolutionary even though the primary point of his ministry does not appear to have been to precipitate a revolution in this area. Women who aspire to a greater fulfillment of their own humanity and those who sympathize with them in this yearning can hardly look for a better ally than Jesus."[14]

WOMEN IN THE CHURCH

It's clear that Jesus had a high view of women, both in His own right and when compared to His contemporaries. Still, critics claim the church denigrates women, welcoming them as fellow believers but giving them a second-class status. In reality Jesus' high view of women also influenced the early church. As with Jesus, when we look at women in the church, the first significant and remarkable fact is that they are *present*. One scholar remarks, "Women are highly visible and active in the life of the church."[15] In other words, women were not just present in the church but were active participants in it. A sampling of the involvement of women in the life of the church as documented in Acts is found in Acts 16:13–15 (Philippi), 17:4 (Thessalonica), 17:12 (Berea), 17:34 (Athens), and 18:2 (Corinth).[16] Women are also featured in several other portions of the New Testament beyond the four Gospels, including the following instances:

- Mary the mother of Jesus and other women are among the disciples in the upper room (Acts 1:14).
- Women are baptized along with men (Acts 8:12; 16:15).
- Women prophesy (Acts 2:18; 21:9; 1 Cor. 11:5).
- Paul preaches to a group of God-fearing women without other men present (Acts 16:11–15).
- In Romans 16 Paul commends several Christians in a list that is approximately one-third women.
- Widows have a special role (1 Tim. 5:2–16).
- Some of the significant women mentioned in the New Testament are Priscilla (Acts 18:18–19), Chloe (1 Cor. 1:11), Nympha (Col. 4:15), Phoebe (Rom. 16:1), Lydia (Acts 16:14), Tabitha raised from the dead (Acts 9:36–42), and Euodia and Syntyche who are called "fellow workers" (Phil. 4:2–3).

Based on the biblical evidence, it's clear that "apostolic churches followed the pattern established by their Lord by including women as integral members. Women attended worship, participated vocally, were taught, learned of the faith and shared it with others. They also played an active part in the daily life of the community, teaching one another and caring for the poor."[17] Furthermore, Paul's words that "as many of you as were baptized into Christ have put on Christ. There is neither Jew nor Greek, there is neither slave nor free, there is no male and female, for you are all one in Christ Jesus" (Gal. 3:2–28 ESV) point to the fact that there is something beyond gender distinctions and roles that binds us all in Christ. Consequently, to treat a woman as inferior is to deny the One who has made and redeemed her.

There are other indicators of the role women had in the early church, such as their involvement in the development and disbursement of Christianity. In fact, the earliest, undisputed reference to Christianity from a non-Christian mentions that Christian women can be deaconesses.[18] As Witherington notes:

> The community of Jesus, both before and after Easter, granted women *together* with men (not segregated from men as in some pagan cults) an equal right to participate fully in the family of faith. That was a right that women did not have in contemporary Judaism or in many pagan cults. Jesus' teachings . . . effectively paved the way for women to play a vital part in His community. *Anyone* could have faith in and follow Jesus—He did not insist on any other requirements for entrance into His family of faith.[19]

Paul, however, is often singled out as having a low view of women, restricting their ability to participate in church and effectively relegating women to second-class status as Christians. While the writings of Paul have without doubt generated much debate about the role of women in the early church in particular and Christianity in general, the passages in which Paul looks positively upon women are often neglected. Phoebe, for example, is commended in Romans 16:1–2. Paul's greeting in Romans also shows that he went out of his way to include women (16:3–16). Paul also makes mention of women who helped in Philippi (Phil. 4:2–3) and women as prophetesses (1 Cor. 11:5). Moreover, agreeing with Jesus, Paul's stance on singleness was incredibly countercultural (1 Cor. 7), as well as encompassing of both men and women rather than being directed solely toward men. Paul also agrees with Jesus regarding matters of divorce (see, for example, Mark 10:11–12 and 1 Cor. 7:10–11).

In light of these facts, it's clear that Paul takes a positive view of women. Setting aside the difficult passages concerning the role of women in ministry—which are laden with many contextual and cultural issues specific to the original audiences—and instead placing Paul's interaction with women against the common view of the day, Paul, like Jesus, can be said to be incredibly pro-women. At the same time, though, it would be wrong to overstate the case by making Paul an early women's rights advocate.

At any rate, given the overall evidence of the New Testament, Christianity elevated and integrated women in the life of the church, especially when compared to common practices in Greek and Roman religions, as well as first-century Judaism.

HOW JESUS SEES CHILDREN

While the chapter is focused on what the Bible says about women, this is a good place to discuss what God says about children. As we have seen in part 1, children are frequently victims of abuse by the perpetrators who abuse women.

In His ministry, Jesus showed striking interest in and love for children, often including them in His teaching, to the surprise of His disciples: "Then children were brought to him that he might lay His hands on them and pray. The disciples rebuked the people, but Jesus said, 'Let the little children come to me and do not hinder them, for to such belongs the kingdom of heaven'" (Matt. 19:13–14). When the disciples came to Jesus asking Him which one of them was going to be the greatest in Christ's kingdom, Jesus called a child to Himself (Matt. 18:2) and said, "whoever humbles himself like this child is the greatest in the kingdom of heaven" (Matt. 18:4). Jesus went on, telling His followers that part of their duty is to receive little children: "Whoever receives one such child in my name receives me" (Matt. 18:5).

Jesus wants His followers to honor, protect, and care for those among them who are small and vulnerable, especially children. Part of Jesus' ministry on earth involved healing children. In Mark 5:39, Jesus came into the house of a ruler of the synagogue, whose daughter had just died. Jesus said that she was not dead but only sleeping. After those gathered laughed at Him, Jesus said to the child, "Little girl, I say to you, arise" (Mark 5:41; cf. Luke 8:54). Mark recounts what happened next: "And immediately the girl got up and began walking (for she was 12 years of age), and they were immediately overcome with amazement" (Mark 5:42). Similarly, in Mark 9, Jesus heals a young boy who had been having demonic attacks. Jesus, who calls Himself "the resurrection and the life" (John 11:25), brings life and healing to children.

The tenderness and care Jesus showed for children is an expression of God's heart toward the small, the weak, and the vulnerable, as seen throughout the Old Testament.

Part of God's law, given at Mt. Sinai, was that no one should "take advantage of the widow or the fatherless" (Ex. 22:22). Indeed, God is one who "defends the cause of the fatherless and the widow" (Deut. 10:18) and curses anyone who perverts the justice due to orphans (Deut. 27:19). The Lord says that no one should do wrong or be violent toward innocent children and orphans (Jer. 22:3). Not only does God want His people to love and care for children, but they are called to do everything in their power to stop those who try to hurt, abuse, or oppress them: "Learn to do right; seek justice. Defend the oppressed. Take up the cause of the fatherless; plead the case of the widow" (Isa. 1:17). Children are a gift from God (Ps. 127:3) and a blessing, and are to be loved, disciplined, and cared for.

WHAT THE BIBLE REALLY SAYS

Far from demeaning women, marginalizing their role, or treating them as inferior to males, the Bible esteems and values women, viewing them as created in God's image and granting them the freedom to actively contribute to the life of the church. As Alvin Schmidt, a sociologist who studied the rise of Christianity, remarks, Jesus' "actions and teachings raised the status of women to new heights, often to the consternation and dismay of his friends and enemies. By word and deed, he went against the ancient, taken-for-granted beliefs and practices that defined woman as socially, intellectually, and spiritually inferior."[20]

After exploring what the Bible says about women, Roger Nicole concludes: "In view of all of the above it is clear that the Scripture provides for women a place of unusual dignity and significance. It never demeans the activities in which primarily women are engaged, such as functioning as wife, home builder, mother, educator of children. To engage in these notable activities according to Scripture is not to choose some second-best option, manifestly inferior to the pursuit of an independent career."[21]

From the beginning, women are created in the image of God alongside of man. As integral parts of humanity, men and women, together, are given the mandate to fill the earth and subdue it (subdue simply means to tame or bring order. Think of a beautiful garden that if not tamed will overgrow and become unruly.). In Christ they both share equal parts of redemption. At the same time, the Scriptures also show and even praise women engaging in roles that we often deem masculine. This is even more striking within the patriarchal culture of the Bible. All of this demonstrates that God's intention in creation and redemption is man and woman working in tandem, both offering their own gifts and abilities (though not always as neatly particularized as traditional views of masculinity and femininity can sometimes make them). In the holy tandem God intended, there is no room for manipulation, power plays, or abusive attempts. There is only mutual love and respect.

This is not to erase creational differences, which should be embraced and celebrated, but to affirm and value both man and woman equally and to highlight the supreme worth and dignity God bestows on the female aspect of humanity, all of which reflects His image and beautiful character.

8

What Does the Bible Say about Violence against Women?

The primary question of this chapter is significantly important, for a reason that psychologist Lenore Walker, in treating patients who have experienced abuse, points out. She says, "Women with strong religious backgrounds often are less likely to believe that violence against them is wrong."[1] Abused women may try to rationalize their suffering by believing that it is "God's will" or "part of God's plan for my life" or "God's way of teaching me a lesson." Yet this image of a harsh, cruel God runs contrary to the biblical image of a kind, merciful, and loving God who promises to be present to us in our suffering—especially when it is unjust.

And this is the true nature of the question at hand. Because to ask what the Bible says about domestic violence is to inquire about the nature of who God is. Is He a God who wields violence as a tool for His punishment? Or is He a God who hates violence and abuse, and grieves its effects on His beloved?

Let's talk a closer look.

THE OLD TESTAMENT ON ABUSE

While some victims of abuse may wonder if the Bible condones their abuse, the Bible actually paints a very different picture. Put simply, God hates abuse, viewing it as sinful and unacceptable.[2]

There are literally hundreds of Scripture passages that condemn abuse and proclaim God's particular judgment on physical abusers.[3] The psalmist, for example, declares God's hatred of abuse in no uncertain terms: "the wicked, those who love violence, he hates with a passion"

(Ps. 11:5). What's more, He promises to judge harshly all unrepentant physical abusers (See Ps. 11:5; Prov. 1:8–19; Joel 3:19; Mic. 3:1–7; Nah. 3:1–7). He despises the plotting of injustice (Psalm 58:2). He will one day punish the violent (Zeph. 1:9). He values breaking "the chains of injustice" even more than displays of piety such as fasting (Isa. 58:4–6). And finally, He calls His people to assertively protect the abused and the vulnerable just as He does (Prov. 24:11–12; Isa. 1:17; Jer. 22:3).

We may already think domestic abuse is certainly a crime against humanity, but the Bible shows us it is also more than that. More than a criminal act, it is a sin that God abhors. When someone defaces a human being—God's image bearer—it is ultimately an attack against God Himself. Ron Clark says it clearly, "Domestic violence is not only a crime against humanity, it is a sin against God . . . To ignore this violence and humiliation is to ignore the voice of God."[4]

The flip side of God's hatred for violence is His inexhaustible concern and care for the oppressed. He not only hates violence and injustice, but He delights in rescuing the oppressed (2 Sam. 22:49).

Throughout the Bible we see this unrelenting concern expressed by God for those who are weak, powerless, and oppressed. There are a few different words for "poverty" in the Hebrew Bible, but the most common is *'ani*, which not only connotes being economically poor but also "oppressed, exploited, and suffering."[5] For example, in the Psalms the *'ani* are "depicted generally as being hounded and seized by the wicked and strong (10:2, 9; 14:6; 35:10; 37:14; 106:16) or being plundered [12:5]."[6] One can see how easily such a description could be applied to include a woman suffering violence from an oppressor. This biblical term is also a helpful one for our understanding, because it encompasses violence that is not only physical but verbal, emotional, mental, and spiritual as well.

Let's consider one particular instance of domestic violence in the Old Testament, in which God executes justice for the victim. In 1 Samuel 25 we learn about a man named Nabal, who Scripture says was "harsh and badly behaved" (25:3). This description of Nabal immediately follows the identification of his wife, Abigail, and so we can infer that she was commonly the object of his harshness. The story says Nabal had greeted David's messengers with insults and inhospitality, provoking David to go to war with Nabal and his house. But Abigail hears of David's plan and begs him not to harm Nabal. Abigail asks David to forgive Nabal, and he complies. However, when Abigail returns and tells her husband what has taken place, "His heart failed him and he became like a stone. And about ten days later the Lord struck Nabal, and he died" (1 Sam. 25:37–38).

This story is told from the perspective of compassion on behalf of Abigail. God saw her in her suffering, and He acted mercifully to her by avenging her perpetrator. Of course God does not always work in miraculous ways such as this, but this story does reveal God's heart of compassion for Abigail in her unjust suffering.

The Bible is full of stories—like Abigail's—in which God actively rescues the oppressed from violence. What's more, He calls us to follow His lead. In Jeremiah 22:3, for instance, we see that the Lord calls His people to deliver the oppressed: "This is what the LORD says: Do what is just and right. Rescue from the hand of his oppressor the one who has been robbed. Do no wrong or violence to the foreigner, the fatherless or the widow, and do not shed innocent blood in this place."

THE NEW TESTAMENT ON ABUSE

The Old Testament certainly sets the stage for God's attitude toward abuse, but what about the New Testament?

First of all, the answer to this question is found squarely at the center of the mission of Jesus—as we are told that He came to set the captives free (Luke 4:17). This includes women who are threatened with violence and abuse.

Consider the story of the woman caught in adultery (John 8). The religious authorities wanted to stone her to death, but Jesus defended her, saying, "Let any one of you who is without sin be the first to throw

a stone at her" (John 8:7). In Matthew 18:6, Jesus also expressly opposes violence against children.

Furthermore, Jesus took the definition of violence to an even
deeper level when He condemned physical violence and verbal violence as equal offenses. In Matthew 5:21, He says, "You have heard that
it was said to the people long ago, 'You shall not murder, and anyone
who murders will be subject to judgment.' But I tell you that anyone
who is angry with a brother or sister will be subject to judgment." But
I tell you that anyone who is angry with his brother will be subject to
judgment." Also, in Matthew 12:36–37, Jesus says, "But I tell you that
everyone will have to give account on the day of judgment for every
empty word they have spoken. For by your words you will be acquitted,
and by your words you will be condemned."

In summary, Jesus' heart for women, children, the poor, oppressed,
and suffering matches the heart of God for the poor and powerless that
we find throughout the Old Testament.

The rest of the New Testament echoes this stance. Just as Jesus condemned verbal abuse, so does James 3:6: "The tongue also is a fire, a
world of evil among the parts of the body. It corrupts the whole person,
sets the whole course of one's life on fire, and is itself set on fire by hell."
Similarly, Ephesians 4:29 reads, "Do not let any unwholesome talk
come out of your mouths, but only what is helpful for building others
up according to their needs, that it may benefit those who listen." Paul,
too, opposes violence: "But now you must also rid yourselves of all such
things as these: anger, rage, malice, slander, and filthy language from
your lips" (Col. 3:8).

The New Testament is careful to warn men specifically against violent tendencies.

In Paul's first letter to Timothy, he says that one of the characteristics of a leader of the church must be that he is not violent but kind
(1 Tim. 3:2–4). Colossians 3:19 continues this idea by teaching that
husbands are not to be harsh with their wives but love them.

Ironically, men who abuse often use Ephesians 5:22—"Wives,

submit yourselves to your own husbands as you do to the Lord" to justify their behavior, but this is taken out of context. The entire passage (Eph. 5:21–33) in fact teaches the *mutual* submission of husband and wife out of love for Christ: "Submit to one another out of reverence for Christ" (5:21). Additionally, the word *submit* does not mean to obey, and it is always a chosen act. Submission cannot be forced, it must be chosen—and it must be mutual in this mysterious dance of marriage.

As a matter of fact, that is what Ephesians 5:23 means: "For the husband is the head of the wife as Christ is the head of the church, his body, of which he is the Savior." When Christ came to earth, He laid aside His heavenly power—voluntarily—for His bride the church. In this sense, "head" does not imply superiority (see 1 Cor. 12:14–19). Ephesians 5:25 says, "Husbands, love your wives, just as Christ loved the church and gave himself up for her." The Scriptures call husbands to love their wives as Christ loves the church—and Christ does not abuse His church. He protects and cherishes it. When a husband abuses his wife, he lies horribly about the character of God and the gospel of Christ.

Referring to Christ's self-sacrificing love for the church, Ephesians 5:28–29 continues this thought: "In this same way, husbands ought to love their wives as their own bodies. He who loves his wife loves himself. After all, no one ever hated their own body, but they feed and care for their body, just as Christ does the church." This is a picture of self-sacrifice, not of domination. The godly husband does not seek to control his wife but nourishes and cherishes her.

As we've discussed, the world and the church both have so often gotten masculinity wrong. Male authoritarianism is not what God intended for men. Pastor and social activist Ron Clark writes, "In domestic violence the problem is that husbands do not act like Jesus or God. A man, who hits, humiliates, rapes, or verbally abuses his wife is acting contrary to the God who created him." In other words, a man who is abusive is abandoning his God-given duty.[7] Instead, Clark notes, God conducts His relationships with the utmost "love, compassion, honor, and mercy," and men must do likewise.[8]

Ultimately, the broad account of Scripture from the Old Testament to the New reveals a consistent thread emphasizing love, compassion, and mercy, while opposing cruelty, violence, and abuse. In light of this, there is quite simply no biblical justification for abuse. To gain an even deeper understanding of why God hates abuse, we must go back even further.

IN THE BEGINNING: PEACE AND VIOLENCE

Abuse against women goes against the biblical concept of *shalom*, a term that means fullness of peace, universal flourishing, wholeness, and delight. Shalom is the vision of a society without violence or fear: "I will grant peace in the land, and you will lie down and no one will make you afraid" (Lev. 26:6). It entails harmonious relationships with both God and others, a profound and comprehensive sort of well-being, and an abundant welfare overflowing with peace, justice, and common good (Isa. 32:14–20).

The original intent of God was *shalom*. The opening words of Scripture tell us, "In the beginning, God created the heavens and the earth" (Gen. 1:1), and He called His creation good. When He created humans, as the pinnacle of His creation, they were named "very good" (Gen. 1:31). Creation was perfect, humans had harmony in their relationship with God and with each other, and all was well. All was *shalom*.

But it didn't stay this way for very long. Genesis 3 records the terrible day when humanity fell into sin and *shalom* was violated.

Adam and Eve violated their relationship with God by rebelling against His command. This was a moment of cosmic treason. Instead of trusting in God's wise and good word (Gen. 2:16–17), they trusted in the crafty words of the serpent (Gen. 3:1–5). In response, the Creator placed a curse on our parents that cast the whole human race into futility and death. The royal image of God fell into the severe ignobility we all experience. This tragic fall from grace into disgrace plunged humankind into a relational abyss.

If *shalom* is biblical shorthand for the way the world is intended to be, then it follows that the greatest enemy of *shalom* is violence. Indeed, "violence" is one of the first words used to describe the decay of the world after sin entered into it: "Now the earth was corrupt in God's sight and was full of violence. God saw how corrupt the earth had become, for all the people on earth had corrupted their ways" (Gen. 6:11–12).

From the first entrance of violence into the world, we see that such violence grieves the Creator. Because of this violent breaking of *shalom,* evil entered the world, and with it, so did abuse. These sins may be understood as an intrusion upon God's original plan for peace. This helps us see the biblical description of redemption as an intrusion of grace into disgrace, or light into the darkness, to reestablish the power of *shalom* over violence. Just as sin and evil is an intrusion on original peace, so redemption is an intrusion of reclaiming what was originally intended for humans: peace.

Theologian Cornelius Plantinga calls this first sin—and all sin to follow—the "vandalism of *shalom*."[9] As a result, both the vertical relationship with God and the horizontal relationship with God's image bearers are fractured. Sin inverts love for God, which results in idolatry, and sin inverts love for others, which results in exploitation and abuse. Such sin works at cross-purposes with *shalom.*

So what does this all mean in the context of domestic abuse? Simply put, when someone defaces a human being—an image bearer of God—it is ultimately an attack being waged against God Himself. Such abuse, whether it occurs emotionally, verbally, physically, or spiritually, is an assault against God's purpose of *shalom.*

MAKING ALL THINGS NEW

Shalom has been violently broken. However, there is good news: God is in the business of making all things new.

God is not standing idly by to watch violence run its course. He will not allow evil to have the final word. His response to evil and violence is redemption, renewal, and re-creation.

The Old Testament prophets spoke widely of a future time when God would put things right again, and when *shalom* would be finally and permanently restored to God's creation. The restoration of *shalom* is frequently united to the coming of the long-awaited Messiah, prophesied throughout the Old Testament. This Messiah would be a suffering servant (Is. 53) and He would bring *shalom* at last.

As we know, God's desire for *shalom* and His response to violence and abuse culminates in the person and work of Jesus Christ. The restoration of *shalom* is fully expressed in the life, death, and resurrection of Jesus, and its scope runs even deeper than the curse of evil in the world today. The cross is God's attack on sin and violence; it is salvation from sin and its effects. The cross really is a *coup de grace*, meaning "stroke of grace," which refers to the deathblow delivered to the misery of our suffering.

Jesus Christ came into this violent world that was shattered by sin, and He suffered a violent death at the hands of violent men in order to save rebellious sinners. He came that He might rescue us from divine wrath and provide instead divine peace, mercy, grace, and love. The sinless one suffered disgrace, in order to bring sinners and sufferers the grace of God.

The cross is both the consequence of evil and God's method of accomplishing redemption. Jesus proves, by the resurrection, that God redeems and heals. He is in the work of redemption today.

Of course, we know evil still exists, and His redemption is not yet fully complete.

Until Jesus returns, we groan (Rom. 8:23) and we grieve (1 Thess. 4:13). Grief is not a sinful emotion but is the result of sin. God and His people have legitimate grief because of sin and the pain it brings. Yet we can also grieve with hope, because we can look to the day when our grief will be banished (1 Thess. 4:13; 1 Cor. 15:55–57). Because of God's redemptive work through Jesus Christ, He will wipe away all of your tears (Rev. 7:17; 21:4).

What Jesus' resurrection began will find its completion in the new creation. The new heavens and the new earth described in Revelation 21:3–5 show us exactly what we have to look forward to:

> Look! God's dwelling place is now among the people, and he will dwell with them. They will be his people, and God himself will be with them and be their God. He will wipe every tear from their eyes. There will be no more death or mourning or crying or pain, for the old order of things has passed away . . . I am making everything new!

What Does the Bible Say about God Delivering Victims?

According to feminist theologian Carol Adams, victims may believe one of two things when it comes to divine deliverance from abuse. First, they may believe that neither God, the world, nor the church protect the weak. Second, they may believe that God, the world, and the church do protect the weak—but only if they are deserving. The result is that a victim often feels either abandoned by God, or that she is being punished by God.[1]

As we've discussed in the last chapter, we believe the Bible teaches that God wishes for your safety. We may know that God's love moves Him to compassion for His people, and that He feels for His people's suffering. But the next natural question is: What does He do about it? How does this deliverance come about?

GOD'S PROTECTION, CARE, AND PATIENCE

First, we must address the concern that one is undeserving of deliverance and protection. In one sense, this is true—it is the very nature of grace to be undeserved. Because we are all sinful people, none of the grace and deliverance we receive is given for the reason that we deserve it. Yet it is freely given. And at the same time, we can do nothing to merit this gift of grace.

For example, Adam and Eve continue under the shelter of God's care after the fall, even though their behavior has done nothing to deserve such care. The question of deserved or undeserved is irrelevant when it comes to grace. And this, because we are all sinful people, is the best of news. It means that God will never withhold His deliverance on account of your behavior. It also means that there is nothing you can do to "earn" such deliverance—and yet, it is freely given anyway.

Suffering—and the need for deliverance—was never intended to be part of God's world. Yet because of the fall, it is very much part of our world. However, as in the story of Adam and Eve, we find God's care and protection from suffering for His children all throughout the Scripture—even after the fall of mankind.

Some of the most poignant examples of God's deliverance include people we might not expect. For example, after Cain killed Abel, God promised to protect him (Gen. 4:13–15).

God also looked out for Hagar, even though she had a child with Abraham who was not the son of God's promise to him. After Hagar upsets Abraham's wife, Sarah, Sarah forces him to send her away, but God took care of her and her son in the desert where they otherwise would have likely died (Gen. 21:14–20).

When Gideon was weak in faith and needed extra proof from God that He would indeed save him and Israel from their enemies, God was patient with him and offered proof (Judg. 6:36–40).

God is especially concerned to care for and protect the weak or marginalized: orphans, widows, the poor, and all who suffer unjust oppression. Again and again throughout Scripture, we see Him responding to injustice on behalf of the oppressed:

- "The Lord is a refuge for the oppressed, a stronghold in times of trouble" (Ps. 9:9).
- "You, Lord, hear the desire of the afflicted; you encourage them, and you listen to their cry, defending the fatherless and the oppressed, so that mere earthly mortals will never again strike terror" (Ps. 10:17–18).
- "May he defend the afflicted among the people and save the children of the needy; may he crush the oppressor" (Ps. 72:4).

- "On the day the Lord gives you relief from your suffering and turmoil and from the harsh labor forced on you, you will take up this taunt against the king of Babylon: 'How the oppressor has come to an end! How his fury has ended! The Lord has broken the rod of the wicked, the scepter of the rulers, which in anger struck down peoples with unceasing blows, and in fury subdued nations with relentless aggression'" (Isa. 14:3–6).
- "If you do not oppress the foreigner, the fatherless or the widow and do not shed innocent blood in this place, and if you do not follow other gods to your own harm, then I will let you live in this place, in the land I gave your ancestors for ever and ever" (Jer. 7:6–7).
- "This is what the Lord Almighty said: 'Administer true justice; show mercy and compassion to one another. Do not oppress the widow or the fatherless, the foreigner or the poor. Do not plot evil against each other'" (Zech. 7:9–10).
- "So I will come to put you on trial. I will be quick to testify against sorcerers, adulterers and perjurers, against those who defraud laborers of their wages, who oppress the widows and the fatherless, and deprive the foreigners among you of justice, but do not fear me," says the Lord Almighty" (Mal. 3:5).

GOD AS LIBERATOR OF THE OPPRESSED

These verses above show us God's exquisite care and concern for the weak. But He also takes it a step further than that, moving beyond compassionate observer to active liberator of the oppressed.

Different words for "rescue," "deliver," and "save" in the Old Testament and New Testament often overlap in meaning. For example, the Greek word for "save" in the New Testament (*sōzō*) can mean both "save" and "deliver." Thus, throughout the Bible we find God liberating, delivering, rescuing, and saving His people—it is a primary theme throughout all of Scripture.

Consider the following examples:

- "Therefore, say to the Israelites: 'I am the Lord, and I will bring you out from under the yoke of the Egyptians. I will free you from being slaves to them, and I will redeem you with an out-stretched arm and with mighty acts of judgment'" (Ex. 6:6).
- "As surely as I valued your life today, so may the Lord value my life and deliver me from all trouble" (1 Sam. 26:24).
- "The Spirit of the Sovereign Lord is on me, because the Lord has anointed me to proclaim good news to the poor. He has sent me to bind up the brokenhearted, to proclaim freedom for the captives and release from darkness the prisoners . . . " (Isa. 61:1).

These themes are, of course, taken up in the life of Jesus as well. He quotes the text above from Isaiah 61 with reference to Himself in Luke 4:17–19, as a statement of His earthly mission:

The scroll of the prophet Isaiah was handed to him. Unrolling it, he found the place where it is written: "The Spirit of the Lord is on me, because he has anointed me to proclaim good news to the poor. He has sent me to proclaim freedom for the prisoners and re-covery of sight for the blind, to set the oppressed free, to proclaim the year of the Lord's favor."

Consider also these passages that show the compassion of Jesus on the poor, oppressed, and sick:

- "Jesus replied, 'Go back and report to John what you hear and see: The blind receive sight, the lame walk, those who have leprosy are cleansed, the deaf hear, the dead are raised, and the good news is proclaimed to the poor. Blessed is anyone who does not stumble on account of me'" (Matt. 11:4–6).

- "God anointed Jesus of Nazareth with the Holy Spirit and power, and how he went around doing good and healing all who were under the power of the devil, because God was with him" (Acts 10:38).

HOW GOD DELIVERS FROM VIOLENCE

The idea of violence in Scripture is a broad one, including physical harm but also other forms of wrong such as the abuse of power, used to oppress others. God's people suffer this kind of violence throughout the history of redemption—they are not immune to it. But they are also promised deliverance from it, and their deliverer is not ignorant of their plight and suffering. He is strong to save and promises that violence does not have the final word in the life of anyone who belongs to Him.

As we've explored previously, the Lord again and again throughout the Old Testament shows His hate for lack of justice and violence against the vulnerable. And again and again, God sides with the injured person against the violent man.[2]

Although God might seem distant, the Bible almost always assumes that salvation comes about because God takes an interest in our lives and acts—albeit sometimes behind the scenes, and many times through the help and compassion of other people. As a matter of fact, deliverance almost always assumes this outside help. This helps us to understand deliverance not as a single miraculous act of God, but through our ordinary circumstances that may include the communal support of those around us and our own personal actions to avoid abuse. This does not mean we can save ourselves, but it does mean proactively choosing to flee violence where it can be avoided, which can aid in the deliverance God is already bringing about.

Deliverance, then, is not something that happens "magically" and only through praying and waiting on God. Rather, it happens in real time, in real circumstances. New Testament scholar Scot McKnight explains,

The focus of the various images for salvation and deliverance in the psalms is on personal deliverance from enemies and life's real troubles rather than, as is often the case in Christian theology, on images of salvation in the afterlife for the individual . . . It is this focus on real-life problems, such as being surrounded by enemies intent on killing the psalmist, that gives to the psalms a potent vision not only of salvation but also of a life of faith, a life of prayer, and a life of petitioning God for deliverance from physical dangers.[3]

The Greek work *sōtēr* means both "Savior" and "Healer." "Sozo" denotes "rescue and deliverance in the sense of averting some danger threatening life."[4] New Testament commentator Leon Morris explains,

Salvation is a general term, denoting deliverance of varying kinds. It may be used of the healing of disease, of safety in travel and of preservation in times of peril. It may apply to people or to things. In the OT, when Israel was threatened by hostile nations, the term is used of God's protection. In the Gospels it is often used of Jesus' healings ("Your faith has saved [i.e., healed] you"). But the term is also used for deliverance from sin and for the ultimate deliverance when the saved enter bliss with Christ at the end of the age.[5]

Sin has been taken care of in Christ, and this is the lynchpin of human history. But it is also true that sin is the ultimate barrier to life in God, which will ultimately be a life of complete wholeness in body, soul, and spirit. Thus, we need two forms of salvation: salvation from our own sins, and salvation from the dangers and violent circumstances in which we find ourselves.

We already know, on a theological level, that the same God who forgives us will one day heal our bodies in the resurrection. So let us also remember, on a practical level, that He is interested in our physical and mental well-being here and now. The bottom line of all of this is that God is a God who delivers His people from all kinds of evil—including violence.

One can walk through the pages of Scripture and see the active reality of God's salvation from violence. Jacob is delivered from Esau, Joseph from the evil intent of his brothers, Moses from Pharaoh's command to kill, the people of Israel from Egypt, then from the Canaanites through Joshua and the judges, David from the Philistines, countless other kings of Israel and Judah from many other enemies, Elijah from Ahab and Jezebel, Daniel from the lions' den, Jonah from the fish, the Ninevites from judgment announced through Jonah, Esther and her people from Haman's plot, the early Christ-followers from demonic oppression and attack through the hand of Jesus and His apostles, and the list continues. The central theme in all this is that God gave Himself for sin, the greatest weapon of the enemy to destroy us, to "deliver us from the present evil age," and this has ramifications for deliverance from all kinds of evil now and into the future. God has been saving and delivering people since the fall of man, and its culmination is Christ's death and resurrection, the centerpiece of all history.

Here are a few other scriptural examples to give a general picture of deliverance throughout the biblical story:

- "Save me, I pray, from the hand of my brother Esau, for I am afraid he will come and attack me, and also the mothers with their children" (Gen. 32:11).
- "The Lord who rescued me from the paw of the lion and the paw of the bear will rescue me from the hand of this Philistine." Saul said to David, 'Go, and the Lord be with you'" (1 Sam. 17:37).
- "As surely as I valued your life today, so may the Lord value my life and deliver me from all trouble" (1 Sam. 26:24).
- "In you, Lord, I have taken refuge; let me never be put to shame; deliver me in your righteousness" (Ps. 31:1).

- "Deliver me from evildoers and save me from those who are after my blood" (Ps. 59:2).
- "Rescue me from the mire, do not let me sink; deliver me from those who hate me, from the deep waters" (Ps. 69:14).
- "Save me, Lord, from lying lips and from deceitful tongues" (Ps. 120:2).
- "Rescue me, Lord, from evildoers; protect me from the violent . . ." (Ps. 140:1).
- "Do not say, 'I'll pay you back for this wrong!' Wait for the Lord, and he will avenge you" (Prov. 20:22).
- "And lead us not into temptation, but deliver us from the evil one" (Matt. 6:13).
- "What a wretched man I am! Who will rescue me from this body that is subject to death?" (Rom. 7:24).
- " . . . Who gave himself for our sins to rescue us from the present evil age, according to the will of our God and Father . . ." (Gal. 1:4).

GOD IS A GOD WHO DELIVERS

Scripture is clear: our God is a God who delivers. However, sometimes the deliverance we hope for does not arrive as quickly as we'd like it to. Therefore, when we do not experience the present reality of deliverance, our hope is in the *promise* of deliverance. There is a present and future reality to all salvation and deliverance. Our lasting hope is deliverance by the strong hand of God, but the hard reality is that this does not always come when or in the way we wish. The mystery of suffering and pain is real.

Scripture offers examples all across the spectrum of those rejoicing in God's deliverance on one end and those crying out for Him to show up on the other. In any given moment of this life, we may find ourselves at different places on the spectrum. But wherever we are, our lasting *hope* is in the deliverance of God.

While we wait and hope, we can do two things: we can look to the future and final deliverance God promises with the return of Christ, and we can actively posture ourselves to avoid violence that is avoidable.

And while we wait, we can find assurance in Psalm 46:1, "God is our refuge and strength, an ever-present help in trouble." David does not promise there will be no trouble or any heartache in this life. He only promises that God is with you in the trouble. The cross and resurrection shows you that God mysteriously pulls you toward Him even as you squirm and resist. And He is there in the dark places when you feel most alone.

Of course, this presents a paradox: How can you feel so alone and yet sense deeply that God is near? David describes the same experience in Psalm 10. He cries out in verse 1: "Why, Lord, do you stand far off? Why do you hide yourself in times of trouble?" But then David declares unequivocally in verse 17: "You, Lord, hear the desire of the afflicted; you encourage them, and you listen to their cry." The laments of this psalm encourage us to risk the danger of speaking boldly and personally to God.

Influential Old Testament scholar Walter Brueggemann reminds us that "the laments are refusals to settle for the way things are. They are acts of relentless hope that believes no situation falls outside Yahweh's capacity for transformation." [6]

The same is true for you today. Your situation does not fall outside God's reach of transformation. Psalm 10 can serve as a prayer for you as you reflect on the temptation of denial and the need for grief and mourning while still hoping in God's healing and restoration.

Does the Bible Say I Should Suffer Abuse and Violence?

T ragically, at least one in four women experiences violence from her partner at some point in her adult life.[1] And tragically, that rate is no different among Christian homes and homes of other faiths or no faith. In fact, research shows that Christian women stay far longer in the abusive context and in far more severe abuse than their non-Christian counterparts.[2]

Women caught up in the cycle of abuse may think, "I can't leave this abusive situation because the Bible says divorce is wrong." Likewise, abusive husbands may claim, "The Bible commands that my wife should be submissive to me."

Abusive men often take the biblical text and distort it to support their right to abuse. We even know of clergy who have said to victims of abuse, "Jesus' wounds were redemptive—they saved the world. Your wounds can be redemptive and save your relationship." Similarly, we know of pastors who have counseled abused women: "If you just submit to your husband, even if he is abusive, God will honor your obedience and the abuse would either stop or God would give you the grace to endure the abuse."

Some have even misapplied 1 Peter 1:6 to the context of abuse: "In all this you greatly rejoice, though now for a little while you may have had to suffer grief in all kinds of trials." This verse has been grossly misused to tell women they should accept abuse and use the suffering as an opportunity to grow their faith.

It is true that people suffer in all kinds of ways. It is also true that Jesus' life, death, and resurrection paint a picture of suffering that leads to glory. This undergirds a central theme found throughout the New Testament that suffering can be redemptive. In fact, Paul says that "Everyone who wants to live a godly life in Christ Jesus will be persecuted" (2 Tim. 3:12), and he told the first churches that "We must go through many hardships to enter the kingdom of God" (Acts 14:22). Certainly suffering has the potential to be purifying and strip us of ingrained attitudes and habits that lead us away from God. It also has the potential to drive us deeper into trust and dependence upon God.

But the problem with the above arguments for staying within abuse is that God never calls us into violence if it can be avoided. We are not called to passively accept every form of unjust pain that comes our way—especially not abuse.

This is not an idea that comes from Scripture. Rather, Scripture shows us a complex and multifaceted view of human suffering, and so we must not be simplistic in our counsel to ourselves and to others who face unjust suffering. Scripture does not encourage people to endure avoidable suffering and it does encourage them to avoid unnecessary suffering. Let us not fall into the trap of thinking that if you decide to take steps to end the abuse, you are being a bad Christian. Remember that Jesus stood up for the dignity of many women when others looked down on them—He gave them not only a sense of self-worth but a practical way out (as He did for the woman about to be stoned in John 8), rather than telling them to become more accepting of their circumstances.

YOU WERE NOT CREATED TO SUFFER

The reason for this goes back to the beginning: you were not created to suffer. Suffering and pain are a result of sin entering the world. While God mysteriously works within the confines of an evil and suffering world, transforming these things for His own purposes, He Himself is good and does not delight in the suffering of the world. He takes "no pleasure in the death of the wicked" (Ezek. 33:11) and does not tempt anyone to evil (James 1:13). Instead, it is from Him that we receive "every good and perfect gift" (James 1:17).

For example, even after Adam and Eve chose to disobey God, He did not abandon the people He created. Though disobedience brought awareness of nakedness and shame, God did not shame the couple further but instead, "The Lord God made garments of skin for Adam and his wife and clothed them" (Gen. 3:21). Suffering, shame, and pain entered a good world through the deceit of the devil and sin of man, but God showed mercy.

At the other end of history, when the end of the age arrives and the kingdom of God is consummated, suffering and death will be destroyed forever (Rev. 21:3–5).

The full arc of Scripture, from beginning to end, tells us this: we were not created to suffer. God is grieved by our suffering and longs for the day when we will be fully delivered from it.

BIBLICAL EXAMPLES OF AVOIDING SUFFERING

What we have seen, then, is that human suffering and pain in themselves do not originate in the character of God and have no place in God's original designs for creation. Because of this, God's people, while accepting suffering that was unavoidable as an act of trust in God, nevertheless avoided and worked around unjust suffering when they were able.

Let's look at some examples throughout the Bible of God's people who choose to flee abuse and avoid suffering:

NOAH

Noah and his family were able to escape the destruction of the flood and avoid imminent death by obeying God and accepting the deliverance He provided:

So the Lord said, "I will wipe from the face of the earth the human race I have created—and with them the animals, the birds and the creatures that move along the ground—for I regret that I have made them." But Noah found favor in the eyes of the Lord. (Gen. 6:7–8)

PATRIARCHS SAVED FROM FAMINE

All three of the biblical patriarchs—Abraham, Isaac, and Jacob—could have died by starvation in their lifetimes because of famine in the land. Each one, however, found a way out that was providentially—rather than miraculously—given to them by God. In other words, God used natural and ordinary circumstances to ensure their safety.

ISRAEL IN EGYPT

In Genesis, God explains to Abraham that his descendants would suffer slavery and abuse in Egypt, but that He would deliver them:

> Then the Lord said to him, "Know for certain that for four hundred years your descendants will be strangers in a country not their own and that they will be enslaved and mistreated there. But I will punish the nation they serve as slaves, and afterward they will come out with great possessions." (Gen. 15:13–14)

Israel did indeed suffer in Egypt, but God did not leave Israel in the hands of their abusers:

> Then the LORD said, "I have surely seen the affliction of my people who are in Egypt and have heard their cry because of their taskmasters. I know their sufferings, and I have come down to deliver them out of the hand of the Egyptians and to bring them up out of that land to a good and broad land, a land flowing with milk and honey, to the place of the Canaanites, the Hittites, the Amorites, the Perizzites, the Hivites, and the Jebusites. And now, behold, the cry of the people of Israel has come to me, and I have also seen the oppression with which the Egyptians oppress them. Come, I will send you to Pharaoh that you may bring my people, the children of Israel, out of Egypt." (Ex. 3:7–10 ESV)

God's rescue of Israel out of the hands of their oppressors in Egypt is a theme that continues through the rest of the Bible. For example, their oppression in Egypt should lead them to have compassion on foreigners in their midst:

> You shall not wrong a sojourner or oppress him, for you were sojourners in the land of Egypt. You shall not mistreat any widow or fatherless child. If you do mistreat them, and they cry out to me, I will surely hear their cry, and my wrath will burn, and I will kill you with the sword, and your wives shall become widows and your children fatherless. (Ex. 22:21–24 ESV)

ISRAEL IN THE TIME OF THE JUDGES

During the era of the judges in Israel, God repeatedly intervened through ordinary people and delivered Israel from those who oppressed her, even after she had fallen into great sin:

> Yet they would not listen to their judges but prostituted themselves to other gods and worshiped them. They quickly turned from the ways of their ancestors, who had been obedient to the Lord's commands. Whenever the Lord raised up a judge for them, he was with the judge and saved them out of the hands of their enemies as long as the judge lived; for the Lord relented because of their groaning under those who oppressed and afflicted them. (Judg. 2:17–18)

DAVID FLEEING FROM SAUL

After David had been anointed king by Samuel and began to rise in the eyes of the people as the leader of the nation of Israel, Saul became jealous and sought to kill him. In response to this threat, David fled:

> Saul sent men to David's house to watch it and to kill him in the morning. But Michal, David's wife, warned him, "If you don't run for your life tonight, tomorrow you'll be killed." So Michal let

David down through a window, and he fled and escaped. (1 Sam. 19:11–12)

Later, David fears for his life and again flees:

But David thought to himself, "One of these days I will be destroyed by the hand of Saul. The best thing I can do is to escape to the land of the Philistines. Then Saul will give up searching for me anywhere in Israel, and I will slip out of his hand" . . . When Saul was told that David had fled to Gath, he no longer searched for him. (1 Sam. 27:1, 4)

ESTHER AND HER PEOPLE

Instead of passively accepting the unjust slaughter that she and her people were about to receive, Esther mustered all her courage, risked her life, and pled her case before the king. This act of courage and refusal to accept a violent fate resulted in the deliverance of the people of Israel from annihilation. Her cousin Mordecai had prompted her,

"Do not think that because you are in the king's house you alone of all the Jews will escape. For if you remain silent at this time, relief and deliverance for the Jews will arise from another place, but you and your father's family will perish. And who knows but that you have come to your royal position for such a time as this?"

Then Esther sent this reply to Mordecai: "Go, gather together all the Jews who are in Susa, and fast for me. Do not eat or drink for three days, night or day. I and my attendants will fast as you do. When this is done, I will go to the king, even though it is against the law. And if I perish, I perish." (Es. 4:13–16)

Through Esther's actions, the Jews were saved:

On the thirteenth day of the twelfth month, the month of Adar, the edict commanded by the king was to be carried out. On this day the enemies of the Jews had hoped to overpower them, but now the tables were turned and the Jews got the upper hand over those who hated them. The Jews assembled in their cities in all the provinces of King Xerxes to attack those determined to destroy them. No one could stand against them, because the people of all the other nationalities were afraid of them. (Es. 9:1–2)

THE WOMAN CAUGHT IN ADULTERY

Jesus intervened before a mob of religious hypocrites stoned a woman for adultery. In addition to protecting her from death, Jesus also speaks graciously to her: "Neither do I condemn you."

Jesus went to the Mount of Olives. At dawn he appeared again in the temple courts, where all the people gathered around him, and he sat down to teach them. The teachers of the law and the Pharisees brought in a woman caught in adultery. They made her stand before the group and said to Jesus, "Teacher, this woman was caught in the act of adultery. In the Law Moses commanded us to stone such women. Now what do you say?" They were using this question as a trap, in order to have a basis for accusing him. But Jesus bent down and started to write on the ground with his finger. When they kept on questioning him, he straightened up and said to them, "Let any one of you who is without sin be the first to throw a stone at her." Again he stooped down and wrote on the ground.

At this, those who heard began to go away one at a time, the older ones first, until only Jesus was left, with the woman still standing there. Jesus straightened up and asked her, "Woman, where are they? Has no one condemned you?"

"No one, sir," she said.

"Then neither do I condemn you," Jesus declared. "Go now and leave your life of sin." (John 8:1–11)

JESUS

It is true that Jesus' life was marked by suffering that He willingly took upon Himself. But the purpose of this suffering was so that we could avoid it—so that He could suffer in our stead. Jesus was motivated to undergo suffering for the very reason that we would be spared.

And even Jesus Himself avoided physical assault by hiding, maintaining physical separation from His abusers, and by eluding them.

Before He was even a grown man, Jesus was whisked away from danger by His family:

> When they had gone, an angel of the Lord appeared to Joseph in a dream. "Get up," he said, "take the child and his mother and escape to Egypt. Stay there until I tell you, for Herod is going to search for the child to kill him."
>
> So he got up, took the child and his mother during the night and left for Egypt. (Matt. 2:13–14)

Later as an adult, He often withdrew from people because He was in danger of physical harm. British scholar R. T. France notes that Matthew repeatedly uses the word *anachōreō*, "depart/withdraw," for Jesus "getting out of a place of danger" (Matt. 2:14; 2:22; 4:12; 12:15).[3] For example,

> But the Pharisees went out and plotted how they might kill Jesus. Aware of this, Jesus withdrew from that place. A large crowd followed him, and he healed all who were ill. He warned them not to tell others about him. (Matt. 12:14–16)

This repeated motif of Jesus' withdrawal is too important to ignore: Jesus is taking precautions to avoid premature confrontation. When the time comes for the showdown in Jerusalem, He will not hold back. But for now He has a wider ministry to fulfill. If controversy is forced on Him, He will respond vigorously, but He takes care to avoid initiating it.

This is the same instruction Jesus gives to His followers: to avoid violence whenever possible. For example:[4]

- "Do not give dogs what is sacred; do not throw your pearls to pigs. If you do, they may trample them under their feet, and turn and tear you to pieces" (Matt. 7:6).
- "If anyone will not welcome you or listen to your words, leave that home or town and shake the dust off your feet" (Matt. 10:14).
- "When you are persecuted in one place, flee to another. Truly I tell you, you will not finish going through the towns of Israel before the Son of Man comes" (Matt. 10:23).

Some other examples of Jesus avoiding abuse are found in John's gospel:

- "'Very truly I tell you,'" Jesus answered, "'before Abraham was born, I am!'" At this, they picked up stones to stone him, but Jesus hid himself, slipping away from the temple grounds." (John 8:58–59)
- "Again his Jewish opponents picked up stones to stone him . . . Again they tried to seize him, but he escaped their grasp." (John 10:31, 39)
- "So from that day on they plotted to take his life. Therefore Jesus no longer moved about publicly among the people of Judea. Instead he withdrew to a region near the wilderness, to a village called Ephraim, where he stayed with his disciples." (John 11:53–54)

Theologian D. A. Carson notes on these texts that "Jesus repeatedly escapes arrest, until the appointed hour of the Father arrives (7:30, 44;

8:20; *cf.* 18:6).ⁿ⁵ In similar fashion, we all have our "appointed hours" of suffering and death, but these are in God's hands, not ours. When we do face suffering, however, we can know that it is God's desire that we be protected. And this protection can involve our own initiative in fleeing harm, as Jesus did.

Just like Jesus' choice to hide Himself from physical threat was part of God's way of protecting Him, so a woman's choice to escape from her abuser is part of God's loving protection.

PAUL

Though he suffered persecution and was eventually martyred, Paul also repeatedly fled from physically abusive civil and religious authorities throughout his life (Acts 9:22–25; 14:5–7; 17:8–10, 14). At one point, Paul would have had the opportunity to endure an unjust and illegal beating for the name of Christ but instead made use of Roman law to avoid it (Acts 22:25–29). About this, John Polhill, a senior professor at Southern Baptist Seminary, writes that "Paul was not about to undergo such torture unnecessarily."[6] New Testament scholar Darrell Bock adds that this passage "indicates that sometimes God can use the governmental systems devised by men to protect Christians. Christians have nothing to fear from systems that seek justice."[7]

On another occasion, Paul made use of a providential situation to avoid suffering and death when his nephew overheard a plot against him (Acts 23:12–13, 16–24).

These passages show that Paul repeatedly fled abusive situations— just as Jesus did. He did not hesitate to use various means to avoid suffering if possible, because he saw this as God's deliverance. Even though Paul was eventually martyred, he never sought out this violent outcome for himself—rather, he took pains to avoid violence altogether wherever possible.

This approach to suffering requires discernment and dependence upon the Holy Spirit, but it also shows that the fundamental human desire to avoid pain is not wrong in itself. In an abusive relationship, there is every reason for a woman to flee and to see this as God's loving means of rescuing her from harm and harm to her children.

HOW TO SUPPORT WOMEN IN THEIR AVOIDANCE OF SUFFERING

What we have seen is that suffering, abuse, and pain are not part of God's original intention for creation, nor for the world to come. One of the best things pastors, ministry leaders, friends, and family can do for a victim of abuse is to assure her of this very truth.

There is a certain mystery in the presence of evil in the world, but the Bible is clear that it does not originate in God. While God's children face all manner of suffering and pain in the world, God is portrayed as one who seeks to protect and care for those suffering, to rescue and liberate those who are oppressed, to be present with them in their pain, and ultimately to redeem everything painful and evil that we suffer. Thus, biblical wisdom calls us to avoid suffering where we can, to make use of the deliverance God provides, and to help others do the same.

In the Bible are numerous stories of godly people repeatedly avoiding abuse and assault by hiding, fleeing from, and maintaining physical separation from an abuser. In the case of domestic abuse, prioritizing protection certainly includes encouraging and supporting women to separate from abusive husbands.

Following these biblical examples, abused women should be encouraged to flee from abusers. Others should assist victims in every way they can to find safety and physical security. We would add that while an abused woman with no children has strong biblical warrant to flee an abusive husband, she has additional warrant to do so if she has children.

This brings us to an important point. Some abused women believe that teaching on the permanence of marriage requires them to stay in an abusive relationship. But no person is expected to stay in an abusive marriage.

Marriage is a covenant; divorce is the breaking of that covenant. When a man chooses to be abusive, he breaks the covenant. An abusive man forfeits the right to remain married unless the woman wants to stay married. If his wife chooses to divorce him, she is making public his breaking of the covenant, and this does not go against what the Bible says about divorce.[8] It is the abuser who must be confronted concerning his or her breaking of the marriage covenant, and "victims need to know that leaving is well within their rights as a child of God."[9]

Abuse, specifically, is a form of oppression that twists God's good intention of marriage. One scholar puts it this way: "Spousal abuse not only violates an individual victim but also ravages the covenant of marriage itself, affecting families, society, and the community charged with sustaining promises of faithful love."[10] If God provides the means to flee and find healing, we should take it—and encourage the same choice for others.

Additionally, clergy or friends should be careful not to use the story of the cross to justify abuse. Marie Fortune, the founder of an interfaith organization dedicated to ending abuse, explains that the cross is not meant to show us that suffering is good—in fact, it shows us just the opposite. She writes,

> Sometimes Jesus' crucifixion is misinterpreted as being the model for suffering: since Jesus went to the cross, persons should bear their own crosses of irrational violence (for example, rape) without complaint. But Jesus' crucifixion does not sanctify suffering. It remains a witness to the horror of violence done to another and an identification with the suffering that people experience . . . The resurrection, the realization that the Christ was present to the disciples and is present to us, transformed but never justified the suffering and death experience.[11]

Fortune also cautions against taking a fatalistic view of God in suffering. Pastors, ministry leaders, and supportive friends and family must take care not to promote the simplistic view that God brought on the abuse for His purposes. This is a distorted view of what is actually happening. Fortune explains, "This 'doormat theology' teaches that it is God's will that people suffer and the only option is to endure it. There is no space to question or challenge the suffering that comes from this injustice, to feel anger, or to act to change one's circumstance." The tragic result of this misunderstanding, Fortune continues, is that the victim is essentially revictimized by her being convinced that she can do nothing to alter her situation.

Ultimately, Fortune says, "There is no virtue in enduring suffering if no greater good is at stake . . . There is no greater good for anyone—certainly not for the victim and children and others who witness the violence but also not for the abuser."[12]

One common reason abused women stay in the relationship is because they believe God wills them to. However, when we realize that allowing oneself to be abused *in no way* furthers to gospel, this argument is made invalid. Abused women are not expected to continue receiving abuse from anyone, especially in a way that enables the sin of their abuser to keep perpetuating itself.

Remember, God's purpose is *shalom*. Violence works at cross-purposes with *shalom*, and He does not want you to suffer under it.

Fleeing from such a person, so that a woman and her children are safe, is a means of deliverance from the Lord. And it is also in the best interest of the abuser, because he is no longer enabled to act out this pattern of sin. The abuser is someone who needs to come to the end of himself to see his need for help. As Fortune writes, staying with them does no good for anyone.

In the end, Scripture does not commend enduring avoidable suffering. There are many biblical examples of godly men and women who made use of practical means to avoid suffering, abuse, and death. Of course we will all face suffering, and inevitably, we will all face death. But it is not up to us to decide when this time is—only God. In the meantime, it is good, right, holy, and wise to work against injustice, to avoid unjust suffering, and to help others do the same.

CHOOSING LIFE—NOT SUFFERING

If you are in an abusive relationship, we know that you are in a complex, dangerous, and desperate situation. When you are in this place, it seems that no choice is easy to make. But we also believe that God has better things in mind for you than to stay in your suffering.

One scholar puts it this way: "It is up to us to choose where we place ourselves: on the side of violence and death or on the side of peace and life. Fatalism and existence doomed to violence are not a part of biblical thinking. As the biblical text exhorts: 'Choose then life, that you may live; you and your children after you' (Deut. 30:19)."[13]

Thus, if a woman has an opportunity to be safe and away from abuse, we believe that God would rather she take the opportunity (please see appendix 1 for many resources on practical steps). More than trying to reform the abuser, staying because marriage is forever, staying to show forgiveness, it is better to be safe.

Part 3

REFLECTIONS
ON PSALMS

11

You Save Me from Violence: Psalm 18

Y ou save me from violence" is an amazing declaration that is found in David's beautiful prayer for deliverance and protection from his enemies in Psalm 18. And it can be your prayer, as well.

This psalm reveals a picture of David's confidence in the power of God—the same powerful and compassionate God who cares about the violence and suffering we experience today. David called on God for the same reason that we can—because evil and violence isn't the way things are supposed to be. And not only that, but God promises that one day He will "make all things new" (Rev. 21:5).

In Psalm 18 David finds himself in trouble—but first, he offers a song of praise to God, recounting the way God saved him from all his enemies. It is a song about a divine rescue from intense trials.

This theme of God saving David from violence (Ps. 18:2, 48; 2 Sam. 22:3, 49) is worth considering from the perspective of domestic violence. It encourages us that despite the evil we may face, our deliverer is not only with us but also has His eye on all those who suffer. Note how God knows and sees the abuse David himself is experiencing within the following psalm. God not only listens to David in his distress; God also springs to action and brings judgment on the oppressor. Though there is trouble all around, the psalmist can still put his trust in the Lord to rightly, and perfectly judge.

Take a few minutes to read this psalm, and find yourself within its narrative:

I love you, O LORD, my strength.
The LORD is my rock and my fortress and my deliverer,
    my God, my rock, in whom I take refuge,
    my shield, and the horn of my salvation, my stronghold.
I call upon the LORD, who is worthy to be praised,
    and I am saved from my enemies.
The cords of death encompassed me;
    the torrents of destruction assailed me;
    the cords of Sheol entangled me;
    the snares of death confronted me.
In my distress I called upon the LORD;
    to my God I cried for help.
From his temple he heard my voice,
    and my cry to him reached his ears.
Then the earth reeled and rocked;
    the foundations also of the mountains trembled
    and quaked, because he was angry.
Smoke went up from his nostrils,
    and devouring fire from his mouth;
    glowing coals flamed forth from him.
He bowed the heavens and came down;
    thick darkness was under his feet.
He rode on a cherub and flew;
    he came swiftly on the wings of the wind.
He made darkness his covering, his canopy around him,
    thick clouds dark with water.
Out of the brightness before him
    hailstones and coals of fire broke through his clouds.
The LORD also thundered in the heavens,
    and the Most High uttered his voice,
    hailstones and coals of fire.
And he sent out his arrows and scattered them;
    he flashed forth lightnings and routed them.

Then the channels of the sea were seen,
  and the foundations of the world were laid bare
  at your rebuke, O LORD,
  at the blast of the breath of your nostrils.
He sent from on high, he took me;
  he drew me out of many waters.
He rescued me from my strong enemy
  and from those who hated me,
  for they were too mighty for me.
They confronted me in the day of my calamity,
  but the LORD was my support.
He brought me out into a broad place;
  he rescued me, because he delighted in me.
The LORD dealt with me according to my righteousness;
  according to the cleanness of my hands he rewarded me.
For I have kept the ways of the LORD,
  and have not wickedly departed from my God.
For all his rules were before me,
  and his statutes I did not put away from me.
I was blameless before him,
  and I kept myself from my guilt.
So the LORD has rewarded me according to my righteousness,
  according to the cleanness of my hands in his sight.
With the merciful you show yourself merciful;
  with the blameless man you show yourself blameless;
  with the purified you show yourself pure;
  and with the crooked you make yourself seem tortuous.
For you save a humble people,
  but the haughty eyes you bring down.
For it is you who light my lamp;
  the LORD my God lightens my darkness.
For by you I can run against a troop,
  and by my God I can leap over a wall.

This God—his way is perfect;
    the word of the LORD proves true;
    he is a shield for all those who take refuge in him.
For who is God, but the LORD?
And who is a rock, except our God?—
    the God who equipped me with strength
    and made my way blameless.
He made my feet like the feet of a deer
    and set me secure on the heights.
He trains my hands for war,
    so that my arms can bend a bow of bronze.
You have given me the shield of your salvation,
    and your right hand supported me,
    and your gentleness made me great.
You gave a wide place for my steps under me,
    and my feet did not slip.
I pursued my enemies and overtook them,
    and did not turn back till they were consumed.
I thrust them through, so that they were not able to rise;
    they fell under my feet.
For you equipped me with strength for the battle;
    you made those who rise against me sink under me.
You made my enemies turn their backs to me,
    and those who hated me I destroyed.
They cried for help, but there was none to save;
    they cried to the LORD, but he did not answer them.
    I beat them fine as dust before the wind;
    I cast them out like the mire of the streets.
You delivered me from strife with the people;
    you made me the head of the nations;
    people whom I had not known served me.
As soon as they heard of me they obeyed me;
    foreigners came cringing to me.

Foreigners lost heart
　　and came trembling out of their fortresses.
The LORD lives, and blessed be my rock,
　　and exalted be the God of my salvation—
　　the God who gave me vengeance
　　and subdued peoples under me,
　　who delivered me from my enemies;
　　yes, you exalted me above those who rose against me;
　　you rescued me from the man of violence.
For this I will praise you, O LORD, among the nations,
　　and sing to your name.
Great salvation he brings to his king,
　　and shows steadfast love to his anointed,
　　to David and his offspring forever.[1]

WHEN VIOLENCE IS THE THEME OF YOUR SONG

The opening verses summarize the theme of the song: namely, that David has found the Lord to be a reliable defender against his enemies. David describes a particular danger that threatened to kill him. In Psalm 18:2 David utters the phrase, "I am saved from my enemies." In 2 Samuel 22:3 (where the same song is found), this phrase is, "You save me from violence."

The word for "violence" in 2 Samuel 22:3 is *hamas*.[2] This is the primary word for "violence" in the Old Testament.[3] But *hamas* is also a highly nuanced term and is not limited to physical violence.[4] It can take on several shades of meaning, including both physical violence and also the sense of "wrong" or harsh treatment.[5] But it always connotes some form of oppression.[6] It even describes a particular commitment on the part of the violent person to bring about the full destruction of the victim. It is, for lack of a better description, the purest form of self-centeredness—it means the violent person will literally stop at nothing to achieve his or her goal. In fact, in many of the Psalms and Scripture's legal literature, *hamas* describes a plaintiff who will stop at nothing to destroy the defendant.[7]

And it is the Lord, in His sovereignty, who alone is able to overcome human *hamas*.[8]

This violence, oppression, and harsh treatment can of course also be carried out by a woman, but in Scripture it is most often used to describe a man.[9] In Psalm 18's parallel song found in 2 Samuel 22, for example, the word "man" (*'ish*) is described as "violent man/men."[10]

A few examples of other uses of *hamas* in the Old Testament are:

- "Now the earth was corrupt in God's sight, and the earth was filled with violence" (Gen. 6:11).
- "The Lord tests the righteous, but his soul hates the wicked and the one who loves violence" (Ps. 11:5).
- "He has pity on the weak and the needy, and saves the lives of the needy. From oppression and violence he redeems their life, and precious is their blood in his sight" (Ps. 73:13–14).
- "Do not envy a man of violence and do not choose any of his ways" (Prov. 3:31).
- "Violence shall no more be heard in your land, devastation or destruction within your borders; you shall call your walls Salvation, and your gates Praise" (Isa. 60:18).
- "Egypt shall become a desolation and Edom a desolate wilderness, for the violence done to the people of Judah, because they have shed innocent blood in their land" (Joel 4:19).
- "Her prophets are fickle, treacherous men; her priests profane what is holy; they do violence to the law" (Zeph. 3:4).

The song found in Psalm 18 and 2 Samuel 22 represent the mortal danger of this violence vividly. David's enemies threaten to overwhelm him. Cords of death threaten to entangle him, and the torrents of the river assailed him (Ps. 18:4). Psalm 18:5–6 depicts this danger as "the picture of death and Sheol as all-engulfing water, and as an inescapable hunter whose traps and nets are ever ready."[11] Violence threatened to

r accusation comes in various forms
riptures—some petty and seemingly
However, in those instances where
t always revolves around His particu-

threatened David, God intervened
ved David through the trial and even-
justice.

ut the history of God's people. God's
oves forward through Israel, and any
ied while following that plan, God
lividuals or groups of faithful follow-
suffering at the hands of violent and
d those who remained faithful and

d moved toward the New Testament,
When Jesus, the great King Himself,
red violence. Given the explicit task
rogram, Jesus was rejected by the
heir malicious attitudes and violence
ilt, subterfuge, and outright attacks
violence of the rebelling people cul-
e the one who claimed to be King
rone of David, His ancestor.

ig. And it is the hope of His resur-
oy which to endure our own trials.
om. 8). And someday, the King will
idication and renewal. In the mean-

ERVION

ower to intervene. The speaker can
t is important to note that nowhere

take David's life, and in distress he called to God (Ps. 18:6). This describes well the experience of many domestic violence victims of being overwhelmed and feeling like they are suffocating. And the next part of David's song gives us hope for rescue.

SAVED

Saved—this phrase is a good summary of David's whole experience with God as laid out in the psalm, where God is referred to as "deliverer," "fortress," "rock," "refuge," "shield," "horn of my salvation," "stronghold," and "savior." He "bows the heavens" and comes down, saving David from the "waves of death" and "torrents of destruction."

The word for "save, deliver" is used often in the Old Testament, and its noun form, "salvation," echoes the names "Joshua" in the Old Testament and "Jesus" in the New Testament, both of which mean "Yahweh is salvation." The idea of God saving is so centerpiece to His nature that it is part of His very name. And throughout the Bible, we see this threaded throughout the entire history of redemption in both the story of Israel and the coming of Jesus for His people.

This word—"saved"—is an important word in David's song. "Saved" and its synonym "delivered" occur 14 times in this song. Eugene Peterson, the mind behind the popular contemporary *The Message* Bible, explains:

> "Deliver" and "save" deeply root David's prayer in God's gracious action. It is common to suppose that first we pray and then God acts; the sequence is reversed here: God acts and then David prays. Both sequences are possible, but this one deserves more prominence than we often give it.[12]

In Psalm 18:1–3, commentator Joyce Baldwin also notes of the God David encounters here that "A torrent of metaphors proclaims to the world that David has found his God to be a rock of ages, utterly dependable in all kinds of dangerous situations . . . [and] is, infinitely resourceful in delivering all kinds of dangerous situations, infinitely re-sourceful in delivering his servant from death."[13] These verses celebrate the reliability of God as a deliverer. In Psalm 18:1 this affirmation is preceded by the confession, "I love thee, O Lord, my strength." The relationship between the psalmist and God is one that is based on love. It is an active relation in life based on full trust and total surrender to God (Deut. 6:5; 10:12; Josh. 22:5).

In these verses, as Pastor Gnana Robinson writes, ". . . The psalmist experiences the reliability of God which he expresses by the use of the images of 'rock,' 'fortress,' and 'stronghold.' 'Shield' is the symbol of de-fense and protection; the psalmist finds his protection in the Lord."[14]

It was out of this deep trust in the deliverance of the Lord that David called "upon the Lord" and was saved from his enemies (Ps. 18:3). However, a loving relationship to God does not make one immune to troubles in this world. Troubles are part of this sinful world—but in the face of troubles, those who suffer find immediate access to the God of love from whom deliverance comes.

In the next few verses, in Psalm 18:7–8 and 2 Samuel 2:8–9, the images shift quickly. These verses speak of God responding to David's danger as if He were an angry dragon. Next God's coming is pictured as a raging thunderstorm or earthquake.

David portrays his rescue (Ps. 18:16–19; 2 Sam. 22:17–20) as if his enemies were swirling waters about to drown him, from which God plucked him and set him on a "broad place," ground that is high and dry. The Hebrew for "broad place" is the opposite of an expression for being "greatly distressed."

Clearly, the rescue has begun.

BECAUSE HE DELIGHTED IN ME

One of the most comforting and powerful lines in the song is Psalm 18:19 and 2 Samuel 22:20: "He brought me out in a broad place; he rescued me, because he delighted in me." The idea of God "delighting" in people is found in a few places in the Bible and refers

or oppressors. This oppression
throughout the course of the S
inconsequential (Prov. 16:29).
hamas provokes God's response,
lar plan for His particular peopl

When malicious individua
and distributed justice. He prese
tually brought the violent men t

This pattern repeats throug
redemptive plan for the world n
time God's people were threate
stepped in. Often in Scripture, i
ers had to endure long periods o
malicious men. Yet God preser
brought them justice.

As the redemptive plan of G
the pattern shifted ever so slightl
set foot on the earth, He too su
of advancing God's redemptive
people He came to rule. Despite
toward Him, He endured the i
to advance the goals of God. Th
minated in the crucifixion, wh
seemed to lose His claim to the

Jesus is no stranger to suffe
rection that gives us the means
Someday, the suffering will end
stand at the finish line offering
time, this truth can give us hope

GOD'S I

Psalm 18 focuses on God's
only cry; all the action is by God

in David's story did the Lord come swooping to his aid, riding on an angel (Ps. 18:10). Storms (Ps. 18:11–14) were sent to deliver others (Josh. 10:11) but not in David's story; God's wind (Ps. 18:15) carved a path through the Red Sea (Ex. 14:21; 15:10), but no such incident is recorded for David. David was delivered by different means: a Philistine raid (1 Sam. 23:26f), the wildness of the terrain (1 Sam. 24:1–3), impressionable conscience (1 Sam. 24; 26), and even by his own fleeing of danger (1 Sam. 27:1).

But this seeming contrast between the terms of this psalm and the terms of David's story is in fact the whole point. When David looked back from the vantage point of deliverance, he tells his story through the lens of God's deliverance of His people in Exodus from the oppression and slavery of the pharaoh.

One scholar explains that David knew deliverance could only have been done by the Lord of Sinai (Ps. 18:7–8) acting in holiness; by the Lord of the judgments on Egypt (Ps. 18:19–12) acting in judgment; and by the Lord of the Red Sea (Ps. 18:15) acting in deliverance. Behind all David's circumstances, David saw the supernatural working of God. So he took refuge in the cave of Adullam (1 Sam. 22:1) and the rocks of the wild goats (1 Sam. 24:2), but in hindsight he saw that it was always the Lord who was his rock and refuge (2 Sam. 22:3, 47).

We wrote on this passage not to give you false hope that you will experience a miraculous deliverance, that your circumstances will change quickly, or that your abuser will suddenly change. We believe and hope that all these things are possible, but unfortunately, they are not likely. We don't want to communicate that the only response to what you are experiencing is to cry out to God and wait for a miracle. While God has and does work in extraordinary means like miracles, He also uses ordinary means to achieve His purposes as He did with David. There is nothing less faithful about crying out to God while also seeking safety, peace, and healing. In fact, David shows us this is a very faithful way to act.

Our hope is that victims, like David, will cry out to God and experience deliverance. We also want you to know and be comforted by the reality that God knows, see, hears, and cares about your suffering. Additionally, God wants you to be safe, healed, and at peace even more than you do. Perhaps knowing this will also encourage you to take steps in this direction.

COMFORT FOR THE AFFLICTED

The theme of God's rescue is echoed all throughout Scripture. God rescued the Israelites from Egypt. He rescued David from his oppressors. And He rescues us from the hand of Satan and the present evil age (Gal. 1:4) through Jesus' life, death, and resurrection.

Why does God do this for us? Because He delights in us (Ps. 18:19; 2 Sam. 22:20). The language of righteousness and blameless is important here. God saves David according to his righteousness, though of course David was not perfect—just as we are not perfect. What makes the difference is that David still sought God, and so can we. Furthermore, on this side of the cross we have the benefit of knowing and receiving the true righteousness of Christ, which *is* perfect. The revelation of the cross gives us even more reason to hope in our righteousness, which is really Christ's righteousness that has been attributed or imputed to us. We should not let our own sin and failures blind us to the righteousness we have, which comes from Christ alone. We can know and trust that we are God's beloved, clean and pure in His sight. God is a rock and refuge and though His presence feels hidden at times, He nevertheless delights in His children, promising deliverance to them as they wait for His coming rescue.

The phrases "I am saved from my enemies" and "you save me from violence" are filled with honesty and hope. Given the meaning of this song and the principle developed throughout the Scriptures and in Jesus' life, we can make the following applications:

1. The abused person can find hope in the King. The promise of resurrection, renewal, and final vindication that comes with the

return of our King gives the abused person this incredible hope for healing.

2. Abuse is neither the fault of the suffering individual, nor the fault of God. Malicious violence (whether physical, verbal, or legal) comes at the hand of wicked men and women. They alone carry the guilt, and they alone will suffer judgment.

3. The suffering may not fully end until the King renews all things. There can be healing, but the scars of our suffering will only completely disappear when the King returns.

4. The King does not abandon His people when they suffer. Just as God protected and defended David throughout his experience, so too may the abused person count on the presence of their Savior. Jesus went through it, and He shares in the pain and the grief (Heb. 5:7–8).

The phrases "I am saved from my enemies" and "you save me from violence" contain the powerful hope that God can and will redeem His people from malicious oppression. This stands for the ancient psalmist, and it stands for you too.

However, the ultimate vindication and healing that God promises lies on the other side of the resurrection. Until that day, the people of God can know that He stands with them through the suffering and the pain. He has not forgotten you. Complete deliverance will come—complete renewal will come—when the King returns. That is where we put our hope. Until then, know that God wants you to be safe, healed, and at peace. In addition to the future hope and healing for which we trust, there is hope and healing that is for right now.

take David's life, and in distress he called to God (Ps. 18:6). This describes well the experience of many domestic violence victims of being overwhelmed and feeling like they are suffocating. And the next part of David's song gives us hope for rescue.

SAVED

Saved—this phrase is a good summary of David's whole experience with God as laid out in the psalm, where God is referred to as "deliverer," "fortress," "rock," "refuge," "shield," "horn of my salvation," "stronghold," and "savior." He "bows the heavens" and comes down, saving David from the "waves of death" and "torrents of destruction."

The word for "save, deliver" is used often in the Old Testament, and its noun form, "salvation," echoes the names "Joshua" in the Old Testament and "Jesus" in the New Testament, both of which mean "Yahweh is salvation." The idea of God saving is so centerpiece to His nature that it is part of His very name. And throughout the Bible, we see this threaded throughout the entire history of redemption in both the story of Israel and the coming of Jesus for His people.

This word—"saved"—is an important word in David's song. "Saved" and its synonym "delivered" occur 14 times in this song. Eugene Peterson, the mind behind the popular contemporary *The Message* Bible, explains:

> "Deliver" and "save" deeply root David's prayer in God's gracious action. It is common to suppose that first we pray and then God acts; the sequence is reversed here: God acts and then David prays. Both sequences are possible, but this one deserves more prominence than we often give it.[12]

In Psalm 18:1–3, commentator Joyce Baldwin also notes of the God David encounters here that "A torrent of metaphors proclaims to the world that David has found his God to be a rock of ages, utterly dependable in all kinds of dangerous situations . . . [and] is, infinitely resourceful in delivering all kinds of dangerous situations, infinitely re-sourceful in delivering his servant from death."[13] These verses celebrate the reliability of God as a deliverer. In Psalm 18:1 this affirmation is preceded by the confession, "I love thee, O Lord, my strength." The relationship between the psalmist and God is one that is based on love. It is an active relation in life based on full trust and total surrender to God (Deut. 6:5; 10:12; Josh. 22:5).

In these verses, as Pastor Gnana Robinson writes, ". . . The psalmist experiences the reliability of God which he expresses by the use of the images of 'rock,' 'fortress,' and 'stronghold.' 'Shield' is the symbol of de-fense and protection; the psalmist finds his protection in the Lord."[14]

It was out of this deep trust in the deliverance of the Lord that David called "upon the Lord" and was saved from his enemies (Ps. 18:3). However, a loving relationship to God does not make one immune to troubles in this world. Troubles are part of this sinful world—but in the face of troubles, those who suffer find immediate access to the God of love from whom deliverance comes.

In the next few verses, in Psalm 18:7–8 and 2 Samuel 2:8–9, the images shift quickly. These verses speak of God responding to David's danger as if He were an angry dragon. Next God's coming is pictured as a raging thunderstorm or earthquake.

David portrays his rescue (Ps. 18:16–19; 2 Sam. 22:17–20) as if his enemies were swirling waters about to drown him, from which God plucked him and set him on a "broad place," ground that is high and dry. The Hebrew for "broad place" is the opposite of an expression for being "greatly distressed."

Clearly, the rescue has begun.

BECAUSE HE DELIGHTED IN ME

One of the most comforting and powerful lines in the song is Psalm 18:19 and 2 Samuel 22:20: "He brought me out in a broad place; he rescued me, because he delighted in me." The idea of God "delighting" in people is found in a few places in the Bible and refers to God's acceptance. Psalm 149:9 says "The Lord takes pleasure in his people." "Takes pleasure" literally means "accepts" and alludes to God's acceptance of propitiation offerings, which is based on the Day of Atonement sacrifices described in Leviticus 16. It is a perfect picture of our relationship to God through Christ. We are accepted because God accepted Christ's sacrifice in our place on our behalf.

Being a member of His people establishes your identity and worth. As Zechariah 2:8 says, "Whoever touches you touches the apple of his eye." "Touching" refers to "harmfully touching" or "plundering" God's elect people. This passage says it is tantamount to injuring God. "Apple of his eye" is a remarkable expression, representing one of the most important and vulnerable parts of the body. To strike a blow at God's people is to strike at God—wounding Him in a most sensitive area. "Apple of his eye" describes something precious, easily injured, and demanding protection. And to God, you are nothing short of precious—you are one He longs to protect.

DELIVER US FROM EVIL

Threatened by malicious enemies throughout his lifetime, David saw deliverance by God over and over again. This was a God who lived up to His name. He proved Himself—over and over—to be the upright judge who administered justice when and where it was due. Such justice, however, did not always arrive on command. David's cry of terror in the first part of the song bears this out, as does his prolonged years of fleeing from Saul, his oppressor.

What we see illustrated in the life of David—and poetically described in this song—is the ongoing theme of trials. In the midst of the trial, when David thought he could no longer hold out against the "river," God came to his rescue as the divine mediator of justice. This pattern defined David's life, which is why this song concludes David's story (Ps. 18 and 2 Sam. 22).[15]

Salvation from violence (or, in the case of *hamas*) describes God's vindication of the innocent in the face of malicious accusers or oppressors. This oppression or accusation comes in various forms throughout the course of the Scriptures—some petty and seemingly inconsequential (Prov. 16:29). However, in those instances where *hamas* provokes God's response, it always revolves around His particular plan for His particular people.

When malicious individuals threatened David, God intervened and distributed justice. He preserved David through the trial and eventually brought the violent men to justice.

This pattern repeats throughout the history of God's people. God's redemptive plan for the world moves forward through Israel, and any time God's people were threatened while following that plan, God stepped in. Often in Scripture, individuals or groups of faithful followers had to endure long periods of suffering at the hands of violent and malicious men. Yet God preserved those who remained faithful and brought them justice.

As the redemptive plan of God moved toward the New Testament, the pattern shifted ever so slightly. When Jesus, the great King Himself, set foot on the earth, He too suffered violence. Given the explicit task of advancing God's redemptive program, Jesus was rejected by the people He came to rule. Despite their malicious attitudes and violence toward Him, He endured the insult, subterfuge, and outright attacks to advance the goals of God. The violence of the rebelling people culminated in the crucifixion, where the one who claimed to be King seemed to lose His claim to the throne of David, His ancestor.

Jesus is no stranger to suffering. And it is the hope of His resurrection that gives us the means by which to endure our own trials. Someday, the suffering will end (Rom. 8). And someday, the King will stand at the finish line offering vindication and renewal. In the meantime, this truth can give us hope.

GOD'S INTERVENTION

Psalm 18 focuses on God's power to intervene. The speaker can only cry; all the action is by God. It is important to note that nowhere in David's story did the Lord come swooping to his aid, riding on an angel (Ps. 18:10). Storms (Ps. 18:11–14) were sent to deliver others (Josh. 10:11) but not in David's story; God's wind (Ps. 18:15) carved a path through the Red Sea (Ex. 14:21; 15:10), but no such incident is recorded for David. David was delivered by different means: a Philistine raid (1 Sam. 23:26f), the wildness of the terrain (1 Sam. 24:1–3), impressionable conscience (1 Sam. 24; 26), and even by his own fleeing of danger (1 Sam. 27:1).

But this seeming contrast between the terms of this psalm and the terms of David's story is in fact the whole point. When David looked back from the vantage point of deliverance, he tells his story through the lens of God's deliverance of His people in Exodus from the oppression and slavery of the pharaoh.

One scholar explains that David knew deliverance could only have been done by the Lord of Sinai (Ps. 18:7–8) acting in holiness; by the Lord of the judgments on Egypt (Ps. 18:19–12) acting in judgment; and by the Lord of the Red Sea (Ps. 18:15) acting in deliverance. Behind all David's circumstances, David saw the supernatural working of God. So he took refuge in the cave of Adullam (1 Sam. 22:1) and the rocks of the wild goats (1 Sam. 24:2), but in hindsight he saw that it was always the Lord who was his rock and refuge (2 Sam. 22:3, 47).

We wrote on this passage not to give you false hope that you will experience a miraculous deliverance, that your circumstances will change quickly, or that your abuser will suddenly change. We believe and hope that all these things are possible, but unfortunately, they are not likely. We don't want to communicate that the only response to what you are experiencing is to cry out to God and wait for a miracle. While God has and does work in extraordinary means like miracles, He also uses ordinary means to achieve His purposes as He did with David. There is nothing less faithful about crying out to God while also seeking safety, peace, and healing. In fact, David shows us this is a very faithful way to act.

Our hope is that victims, like David, will cry out to God and experience deliverance. We also want you to know and be comforted by the reality that God knows, see, hears, and cares about your suffering. Additionally, God wants you to be safe, healed, and at peace even more than you do. Perhaps knowing this will also encourage you to take steps in this direction.

COMFORT FOR THE AFFLICTED

The theme of God's rescue is echoed all throughout Scripture. God rescued the Israelites from Egypt. He rescued David from his oppressors. And He rescues us from the hand of Satan and the present evil age (Gal. 1:4) through Jesus' life, death, and resurrection.

Why does God do this for us? Because He delights in us (Ps. 18:19; 2 Sam. 22:20). The language of righteousness and blameless is important here. God saves David according to his righteousness, though of course David was not perfect—just as we are not perfect. What makes the difference is that David still sought God, and so can we. Furthermore, on this side of the cross we have the benefit of knowing and receiving the true righteousness of Christ, which *is* perfect. The revelation of the cross gives us even more reason to hope in our righteousness, which is really Christ's righteousness that has been attributed or imputed to us. We should not let our own sin and failures blind us to the righteousness we have, which comes from Christ alone. We can know and trust that we are God's beloved, clean and pure in His sight. God is a rock and refuge and though His presence feels hidden at times, He nevertheless delights in His children, promising deliverance to them as they wait for His coming rescue.

The phrases "I am saved from my enemies" and "you save me from violence" are filled with honesty and hope. Given the meaning of this song and the principle developed throughout the Scriptures and in Jesus' life, we can make the following applications:

1. The abused person can find hope in the King. The promise of resurrection, renewal, and final vindication that comes with the

return of our King gives the abused person this incredible hope for healing.

2. Abuse is neither the fault of the suffering individual, nor the fault of God. Malicious violence (whether physical, verbal, or legal) comes at the hand of wicked men and women. They alone carry the guilt, and they alone will suffer judgment.

3. The suffering may not fully end until the King renews all things. There can be healing, but the scars of our suffering will only completely disappear when the King returns.

4. The King does not abandon His people when they suffer. Just as God protected and defended David throughout his experience, so too may the abused person count on the presence of their Savior. Jesus went through it, and He shares in the pain and the grief (Heb. 5:7–8).

The phrases "I am saved from my enemies" and "you save me from violence" contain the powerful hope that God can and will redeem His people from malicious oppression. This stands for the ancient psalmist, and it stands for you too.

However, the ultimate vindication and healing that God promises lies on the other side of the resurrection. Until that day, the people of God can know that He stands with them through the suffering and the pain. He has not forgotten you. Complete deliverance will come—complete renewal will come—when the King returns. That is where we put our hope. Until then, know that God wants you to be safe, healed, and at peace. In addition to the future hope and healing for which we trust, there is hope and healing that is for right now.

12

Will God Remain Faithful?: Psalm 22

Have you ever wondered—or even demanded—to know that God is really there? That He truly sees you in your distress?

If so, you're in good company. Psalm 22 contains some of the most heart-wrenching cries to God recorded in all of the Psalms, and they come from the man God Himself called a man after His own heart (1 Sam. 13:14).

In Psalm 22, God Himself is on trial and David asks, "Will God remain faithful?" This is the plea of a believer who wonders where God is. It is a psalm in which the psalmist, in the throes of injustice, wonders if God Himself will be faithful to His promise.

This is a psalm in three movements. The first movement is written with the dark, minor notes of pain, bewilderment, and betrayal. The second movement is written in the bright, major chords of rejoicing and freedom. Finally, the third movement is composed of both the deep, sundering bass notes of God's power and the high ring of celestial praise. The song—intended to be sung on the Sabbath—is a reminder. Like most psalmic worship, David's goal was to weekly remember God's faithfulness to His covenant promises and to reassure others that God's faithfulness was completely trustworthy. Let's listen.

> My God, my God, why have you forsaken me?
> Why are you so far from saving me, from the words of my
> groaning?
> O my God, I cry by day, but you do not answer,
> and by night, but I find no rest.

Yet you are holy,
>   enthroned on the praises of Israel.
In you our fathers trusted;
>   they trusted, and you delivered them.
To you they cried and were rescued;
>   in you they trusted and were not put to shame.
But I am a worm and not a man,
>   scorned by mankind and despised by the people.
All who see me mock me;
>   they make mouths at me; they wag their heads;
"He trusts in the LORD; let him deliver him;
>   let him rescue him, for he delights in him!"
Yet you are he who took me from the womb;
>   you made me trust you at my mother's breasts.
On you was I cast from my birth,
>   and from my mother's womb you have been my God.
Be not far from me,
>   for trouble is near,
>   and there is none to help.
Many bulls encompass me;
>   strong bulls of Bashan surround me;
>   they open wide their mouths at me,
>   like a ravening and roaring lion.
I am poured out like water,
>   and all my bones are out of joint;
>   my heart is like wax;
>   it is melted within my breast;
>   my strength is dried up like a potsherd,
>   and my tongue sticks to my jaws;
>   you lay me in the dust of death.
For dogs encompass me;
>   a company of evildoers encircles me;
>   they have pierced my hands and feet—

I can count all my bones—
>   they stare and gloat over me;
>   they divide my garments among them,
>   and for my clothing they cast lots.
But you, O LORD, do not be far off!
>   O you my help, come quickly to my aid!
Deliver my soul from the sword,
>   my precious life from the power of the dog!
>   Save me from the mouth of the lion!
You have rescued me from the horns of the wild oxen!
I will tell of your name to my brothers;
>   in the midst of the congregation I will praise you:
You who fear the LORD, praise him!
>   All you offspring of Jacob, glorify him,
>   and stand in awe of him, all you offspring of Israel!
For he has not despised or abhorred
>   the affliction of the afflicted,
>   and he has not hidden his face from him,
>   but has heard, when he cried to him.
From you comes my praise in the great congregation;
>   my vows I will perform before those who fear him.
The afflicted shall eat and be satisfied;
>   those who seek him shall praise the LORD!
>   May your hearts live forever!
All the ends of the earth shall remember
>   and turn to the LORD,
>   and all the families of the nations
>   shall worship before you.
For kingship belongs to the LORD,
>   and he rules over the nations.
All the prosperous of the earth eat and worship;
>   before him shall bow all who go down to the dust,
>   even the one who could not keep himself alive.

Posterity shall serve him;
    it shall be told of the Lord to the coming generation;
They shall come and proclaim his righteousness to a people
    yet unborn,
    that he has done it.

CONFLICT: IS GOD FAITHFUL? (PS. 22:1–18)

David most likely composed this psalm while on the run from Saul, so the psalm begins in a very dark place. He had been promised the throne of Israel and the protection of God, yet he had spent the last few years of his life on the run as a fugitive. So David, expressing the very cry of Jesus on the cross, addresses God: "Why have you forsaken me?"[1]

To David, it truly seemed like God had forsaken him and forgotten His promise. David's trouble never seemed to end. And it seemed that God had stopped paying attention.

Yet this situation, David cries, is out of character with God. His holiness and glory have not been jeopardized but are still upheld by Israel. So He cannot have lost His power, David reasons. In fact, when the people of Israel cried out to God, they were rescued and not put to shame. They trusted in God and He answered their cries. So David's next question is, "Why, if you redeemed Israel out of Egypt and her slavery, have you forgotten me?" Over the next few verses, David compares his situation and character to that of Israel. In verses 6–8, he describes his reality: he is despised by his own people, while Israel was only despised by foreigners. In fact, even the people mocking him realize the conflict—they mock him because they believe God will *never* rescue him. And David would like to prove them wrong.

David's frustration mounts in verses 9–11. If God is faithful to His promises to those who are obedient, David has more claim than anyone. As David poetically describes, he was God's from birth. If there is anyone who has a right to call on God's faithfulness, it is David. At this point, God is without an excuse and David's question is simply,

"What gives?" The psalm then relays David's resignation in vivid imagery: he is "poured out like water," even starving to death. David has nothing left to hold out for. His enemies surround him like lions and dogs. The wealth he had before becoming an outcast is divided up among his enemies.[2]

This movement concludes with the final cry of a dying man pleading for God to deliver. David has made his argument and can do no more. He must now wait on God's answer.

This movement should be the heart cry of every believer in the pit of suffering. There is nothing wrong with the tension of asking "Will God be faithful?" Often this question drives believers to worship and anticipates the future action of God. It is part of worship. However, worshipers find hope when they remember the past actions of God.

RESOLUTION: GOD IS FAITHFUL (PS. 22:19–26)

Just when it seems that God has truly gone silent, David's tone changes. In verse 21, his plea—"deliver my soul from the sword"—takes a sharp turn into rejoicing, "You have rescued me." There is no comment as to whether or not David received the redemption for which he longed, but he does here express confidence that God will be faithful to His word. The deliverance found here in verses 19–21 form the foundation for David's praise. It shows us that praise to God for deliverance is not a private act but a communal one. This song, sung among the assembled people on Sabbath, recounts the actions of God in David's life to the people of Israel. The song's praise to God for His intervention reminds the nation of God's acts on the whole nation's behalf. Just as David was redeemed, so was Israel. Just as David has a reason to praise God, so does the congregation. And now, centuries later, these promises stand just as true for you today.

The conclusion to this movement is rather simple despite the terror of the previous movement. The afflicted can trust God for deliverance (verses 24, 26), and this deliverance should prompt obedience. Just as God was faithful to His promise, David promises faithfulness to his own promise (verse 25). Worship, then, is the beginning of obedience.

The next movement concludes the psalm with a thunderous crescendo.

Take a moment to read again verses 27–31 above. The song concludes with a movement so profound it makes the suffering recounted in the first verses seem far away and long ago. Here, David envisions the worshiping of God to expand to all the nations of the world. These nations will *remember* the actions of God—demonstrated in the lives of the people of Israel and her king—and turn to Him in worship. God is truly King over the whole earth and rightly deserves the worship of all people. Everyone—prosperous or otherwise—will serve Him.

Just as a pebble tossed into a lake spreads ripples over the whole lake, a person who experiences God's redemption and praises Him sets off a reaction. The people of God take up the chorus and praise God along with the redeemed, for they too were redeemed. When all the people of God are doing this, they are a witness to God's redemption and an example for the world.

The people of God stand as a powerful witness to the world when worshiping Him for His faithfulness and redemption. Just as Jesus suffered and felt the abandonment of God, yet experienced deliverance to the heights of glory, so Christians can praise God and trust Him for deliverance as they face suffering.

PSALM 22 AND JESUS' SUFFERING

Social justice advocate Marie Fortune writes,

A religious person who is victimized by rape, battering, or child sexual abuse frequently faces the questions, *Why do I suffer in this way?* and, *Where is God in my suffering?* These profound theological questions cannot be answered simply with platitudes and then dismissed. The question of why there is suffering at all is one of classic theological debate, that is, the question of theodicy, to which there is no completely satisfactory answer. Human suffering in the midst of a world created by a compassionate and loving God is a dimension of human experience which is most disturbing and disquieting.[3]

These are not easy questions, as you know. And Fortune is right— platitudes cannot satisfy them. But comfort can be found in the knowledge that you are not the only one to ask these questions. If you find yourself identifying with David in his pleas to God, you are not alone. So did Jesus. In fact, it was during His crucifixion that Jesus quoted Psalm 22 in reference to His own suffering.

Certainly, easy answers and platitudes cannot speak to the answer for the "why" of suffering. But perhaps the cross can. Because whatever pain and suffering you are experiencing right now, Jesus has also faced. He knows intimately the depth of desperation you are feeling.

But this is the crucial difference: He suffered so that you wouldn't have to.

Perhaps no Christian concept is so thoroughly misapplied toward and by victims of abuse than that of Christ's suffering. Too often, Christians believe that because Christ suffered, they too must suffer to become like Him. In terms of domestic abuse, victims sometimes believe their submission to abuse is modeled after Christ's sacrificial love—as a means of making their struggle meaningful. In her mind, how else can she account for her undeserved suffering?[4]

In response to this, feminist theologian Carol Adams argues that no one can save the abuser from his own violent actions. In fact, as she explains, this attempt at misguided redemption will actually backfire: "Whereas Christ's suffering may be seen as redemptive, suffering from abusive men does not redeem, indeed it guarantees that the violence will continue."[5]

Those suffering abuse are free to name sin for what it is without having to spiritualize their own suffering. If you are being abused, name it for what it truly is. The psalmist tells the truth about his own betrayal and abuse, and so should you.

13

But I Will Trust in You: Psalm 55

One of the most common laments in Scripture includes prayers to God to protect the writer from enemy harm. And while Psalm 55 follows this literary pattern, it also carries a unique twist—making it especially relevant for sufferers of domestic abuse.

Because here, the enemy posing harm to the psalmist is named as a "companion" and "familiar friend" (verse 13).[1] Psalm 55 is a psalm of betrayal by someone close to the writer, which correlates closely to the victim's experience of intimate partner violence.

Its themes can help provide a way forward for those who have faced this unique pain.

The psychological and emotional effects of domestic violence—such as depressive hopelessness, lack of self-confidence, and damage to the identity—closely match the feelings depicted in Psalm 55.

As you read through the psalm, you will see how the psalmist's emotions run high. He is desperately afraid and cries continuously to God for help. His distress is particularly sharp because of the betrayal by a person who at one time had been his best friend. At times almost incoherent with despair and rage, the psalmist in the most violent terms prays for the immediate death of his enemies.[2] Yet the psalm is also hopeful—even amid despair, David turns to God in trust, knowing that it is He who fights for him and who sees all injustice and promises to right all wrongs in His own time.

Take a few moments to read and see for yourself.

PSALM 55

Give ear to my prayer, O God,
>   and hide not yourself from my plea for mercy!
Attend to me, and answer me;
>   I am restless in my complaint and I moan,
because of the noise of the enemy,
>   because of the oppression of the wicked.
For they drop trouble upon me,
>   and in anger they bear a grudge against me.
My heart is in anguish within me;
>   the terrors of death have fallen upon me.
Fear and trembling come upon me,
>   and horror overwhelms me.
And I say, "Oh, that I had wings like a dove!
>   I would fly away and be at rest;
yes, I would wander far away;
>   I would lodge in the wilderness; Selah
I would hurry to find a shelter
>   from the raging wind and tempest."
Destroy, O Lord, divide their tongues;
>   for I see violence and strife in the city.
Day and night they go around it
>   on its walls,
and iniquity and trouble are within it;
>   ruin is in its midst;
oppression and fraud
>   do not depart from its marketplace.
For it is not an enemy who taunts me—
>   then I could bear it;
it is not an adversary who deals insolently with me—
>   then I could hide from him.
But it is you, a man, my equal,
>   my companion, my familiar friend.

We used to take sweet counsel together;
    within God's house we walked in the throng.
Let death steal over them;
    let them go down to Sheol alive;
    for evil is in their dwelling place and in their heart.
But I call to God,
    and the LORD will save me.
Evening and morning and at noon
    I utter my complaint and moan,
    and he hears my voice.
He redeems my soul in safety
    from the battle that I wage,
    for many are arrayed against me.
God will give ear and humble them,
    he who is enthroned from of old, Selah
because they do not change
    and do not fear God.
My companion stretched out his hand against his friends;
    he violated his covenant.
His speech was smooth as butter,
    yet war was in his heart;
his words were softer than oil,
    yet they were drawn swords.
Cast your burden on the LORD,
    and he will sustain you;
he will never permit
    the righteous to be moved.
But you, O God, will cast them down
    into the pit of destruction;
men of blood and treachery
    shall not live out half their days.
But I will trust in you.

Derek Kidner breaks up the psalm in the following way, which will be the template followed in this chapter:

> The intolerable strain (verses 1–3)
> The urge to escape (verses 4–8)
> The forces of anarchy (verses 9–11)
> The false friend (verses 12–15)
> The God who hears (verses 16–19)
> The smooth talker (verses 20–21)
> The long view (verses 22–23)[3]

THE INTOLERABLE STRAIN:
VERSES 1–3 ("HEAR MY PRAYER")

The prayer is earnest, and its occasion desperate. The enemy is said to "drop trouble upon me"—as if they were throwing stones—because "they bear a grudge against me." As usual in the Psalms, these are not simply people who dislike the psalmist; they are enemies of true piety, who will even take violent measures to ruin the godly and stamp out true faith (verses 3, 9–11, 21, 23).

This first section begins with a plea to God not to hide Himself. This expression, Kidner notes, echoes the law of Deuteronomy 22:1–4, "by using this very expression to forbid the ignoring of a neighbor's predicament, however inconvenient the moment. So the allusion makes David's prayer an appeal to God's self-consistency as well as to His mercy."[4] As the Israelite was to help his brother when he was in need, David appeals to God to "hide not yourself" in his own time of need.

"Attend to me" is a rather old-fashioned form of English, meaning simply to listen or pay attention. When the psalmist asks God to "answer" him, this does not mean an answer in response to a question. But rather it refers to an answer in terms of action on behalf of the distressed—because things are only getting worse.

John Goldingay, an Episcopal priest who writes on the Old Testament, summarizes these verses well: "Friends are people who would want to keep harm firmly away from us, but these are people who push it to the edge of the roof so that it falls down on us as we stand below."[5]

In other words, this "friend" is treating the psalmist in the exact opposite way one would expect treatment from a friend—a deep betrayal indeed.

THE URGE TO ESCAPE:
VERSES 4–8 ("I AM DESPERATE")

This section describes more fully the earnestness of the singer: "in anguish," "terrors of death," "fear," "trembling," and "horror" are all used to describe his situation. If he could "fly"—the "dove" is probably a symbol of both innocence and swiftness—he would take refuge "in the wilderness" away from the "raging" in the city where his enemies plot against him.

Verses 4–8 provide consolation that we are not alone in our pain and our desire to flee from trouble. And you are not alone in seeking refuge from the abuse and violence within your home.

THE FORCES OF ANARCHY:
VERSES 9–11 ("DESTROY THOSE WHO BRING SUCH RUIN")

In these verses, we find that "in the city all kinds of party passions have broken loose; even his bosom friend has taken a part in this hostile rising."[6] Furthermore, "while any good citizen is distressed at social breakdown, David as king is directly challenged." As such, David prays for God to remember His dealings with other sinful cities. Again, David shows us how to pray by appealing to God's sense of justice and how He has dealt with evil in the past.

This picture of the city is the opposite of its true function—that of protection. German theologian Ulrike Bail explains, "The city, to which the connotations 'protection and safety' should be attributed, no longer offers a place of refuge; instead, it has become profoundly unsafe."[7] The same could be said about friendship and intimate relationships. They are to be places of compassion, care, and love—not threat, harm, and violence.

This is why David's desire to flee is so striking. The psalmist wants to escape from the enclosed space of violence—which should have been a place for refuge—and flee to the desert, which was commonly understood as a place of danger and even death.[8]

Just as the city is intended to be a safe, life-giving place of refuge, so are human relationships—although both can be distorted. Both, as anyone in an abusive relationship knows, can be turned into a place of hopelessness. But hope can be found in surprising places.

To David, that surprising place is the desert. The desert becomes the place of refuge where violence no longer threatens. As one commentator notes, "The desert offers asylum to outcast and refugees. Hagar, Moses, David, Elijah, and others fled into the desert. Here they were met by God or by God's messengers who gave them nourishment, strengthened and protected them."[9]

Here in the desert, the psalmist prays for deliverance and for the thwarting of the wicked schemes of the enemies. The singer would prefer that the enemies repent of their evil; but here seems to expect that they will not (Ps. 55:19).

THE FALSE FRIEND:
VERSES 12–15 ("I AM BETRAYED BY MY OWN FRIEND")

In this section, the pain sharpens: it is not a nameless "adversary" who is seeking to harm the pious singer but "my companion, my familiar friend." The psalmist now speaks of a former friend who has betrayed him. The worst thing about the psalmist's situation is that he is being reviled and mocked by one who used to be an "equal, a companion, a familiar friend." This evokes closeness, trust, and shared experience. The betrayal stings so much because the perpetrator was in a close relationship of trust with the victim. The evil perpetrated was an abuse of this closeness.[10]

The perpetrator is what many have called "the false friend."[11] We don't know specifically which individual David is referring to here, but we do know that David knew about betrayal. He was betrayed by his son Absalom (2 Sam. 15:1–12; 16:15–23) and by his counselor Ahithophel (2 Sam. 15:12; 16:15–23)."[12] Additionally, David may have provided this psalm for God's people to sing under this kind of duress, without being strictly autobiographical.

In verse 15, the psalmist now prays that sudden death come upon his enemies. The psalmist wants them to die at once—before their appointed time.

In verse 15, David suddenly switches from the singular "enemy" to plural "enemies." This may reflect that the friend-turned-enemy was the leader of a group who likewise turned against David, or as one commentator notes, that the "repetition of the various synonyms for 'friend' expresses the severity of the accusation of the treacherous companion."[13]

The idea of going down "to Sheol alive" conjures up an image of being suddenly swallowed alive by the earth—in what would have to be an act of God.

This is a striking image, so let's consider it deeper. Praying for the perpetrator's death reflects an attempt to resist and break the perpetrator's power. The suffering is so intense that only death seems appropriate for bringing an end to the violence, because only through death is reality reversed.[14] Praying for death, in this way, is an expression of the depth of the victim's despair and sense of powerlessness. From David's perspective, it seems that only the perpetrator's death can bring an end to the violence. However, despite his intense feelings on the subject, David gives the matter over to God. He trusts God to act and deal with the perpetrator Himself.

This prayer is a request to God that the dominant discourse of violence be perverted, interrupted, made powerless, and demolished.

What does this difficult passage mean for you in your situation? First, it certainly does not mean that your abuser's death is the only way to end the violence. But David's prayer does show us how to appeal to

God in our distress: to ask Him to deal justly with the perpetrator of
our injustice.

THE GOD WHO HEARS:
VERSES 16–19 ("I CALL TO GOD AND TRUST HE WILL HEAR ME")

Verse 16 signals a pivotal moment in the psalmist's distress: "In
driving God's servant to prayer the enemy has already overreached
himself; a fact worth remembering in such a situation. It is the turning
point of the psalm."[15]

Verse 18 declares an incredible hope: "He redeems." Here, we
catch a glimpse of David appealing to God's rescuing nature. "Redeem"
generally conveys the idea of rescue and protection, especially when
its object is Israel (Pss. 44:26; 111:9; 130:7–8) or a faithful worshiper
(Pss. 34:22; 55:18; 71:23).

David's prayers at "evening and morning and noon" indicate the
regular hours of Hebrew prayer, indicating David's faithfulness even in
the midst of his oppression.

These verses highlight the need to call to God for help in the midst
of this kind of pain and betrayal. In our most raw and wounded state,
this might not be possible. And then, we simply need to be honest and
lament our suffering before God, as David did. But eventually, if we are
to continue forward with God, there comes a time when a ray of light
breaks in that allows us to surrender our hearts to the only one who can
help. It is often at this point that hope begins to dawn more fully, as our
prayers mysteriously work with the purpose of God to bring about our
deliverance—even while we wait in patience and endurance.

THE SMOOTH TALKER:
VERSES 20–21 ("MY TREACHEROUS FRIEND")

This section returns to describing a painful betrayal as the psalmist
refers again to his former friend. This is not simply a friend who has let
another down; he has planned destruction of those who had trusted
him all along. In fact, he had entered the friendship "covenant" all the

while disguising his evil intent. The reference to this covenant signifies that this was no casual friendship—this was a relationship to which both parties had made solemn pledges.

The violence perpetrated is both physical (verse 20) and verbal (verse 21). The focus of verse 20 turns back again to the betrayer who "attacked"—or, sent out his hand against—his friends, literally "those who were at peace with him" or "those who have a covenant with him." The severity of the treachery is seen in the fact that, as Goldingay writes, "it broke specific pledges; it stabbed sworn allies in the back, not merely companions. The sacredness of a *covenant* comes out in the word for *violated*, which means profaning something holy. God would have been invoked as witness to such a bond."[16]

For this reason, the psalmist accuses his former friend of hypocrisy in verse 21. He says the former friend's words were "smooth as butter"—connoting also images of healing oil as applied to a wound. But those words soon turned out to be verbally abusive. David comes to the sickening realization here that language has extraordinary power —a power that can bring death in the same way as weapons.

THE LONG VIEW:
VERSES 22–23 ("CAST YOUR BURDEN ON THE LORD")

The singer addresses each of his fellow singers and then God Himself. "Cast your burden on the Lord" can also be translated "Leave your trouble with the Lord," "Give the Lord your troubles," and "Put on the Lord your troubles." Other ways of capturing this idea are "The Lord will be troubled for you" or "The Lord will have worries in your place." However translated, these words carry powerful comfort for us in dark times.

The reason the faithful can "cast" their "burden on the Lord" is that He can be trusted to bring judgment upon the evildoers. The Psalms do not say when God will "cast them down," but the faithful will wait for God's own good timing.

Finally, in the closing verses of this psalm, we see the singer's confidence that God will answer his prayer.

One scholar writes on verse 23:

> The psalm closes . . . with the petitioner's reaction to the activity of foes and friend: an intensive plea to God to bring both friend and foe to death. From a feminist point of view a special closeness to women's experience can be detected: The experience of violence to which the petitioner is exposed is one of absolute powerlessness. From this perspective of powerlessness, it appears that only the death of her attacker can bring an end to the violence.[17]

We are not encouraging you to pray for the death of your abuser. We are encouraging you, like David, to entrust judgment of your abuser to God alone. Maybe you relate to the intensity of David's fear and pain after being betrayed and harmed by a close companion. If anything, the psalmist's honesty should encourage those who have been abused to be honest with God in the same way. God knows. He sees. And He will bring justice, as He sees fit. That is what we can take away from this psalm.

Commentators highlight the connection of "cast your burden on the LORD" (verse 22) with 1 Peter 5:7, "Cast all your anxieties on him, because he cares for you." The language is very similar. Thus, while there may be a place for calling for justice of those who violently wrong us, we must still leave vengeance to the Lord (Rom. 12:19). David never forgets "that this is of God's appointment, whose world this is . . . What counts is that God has the whole matter in hand, and that David's choice has been made."[18] He will trust the Lord, even as he longs for and calls out for justice.

And in the meantime, God "sustains" those who wait on Him. He offers support and provides for one's needs. Acknowledging this, David is able to close this psalm with the final resounding phrase: "But I will trust in you."

I WILL TRUST IN YOU

No doubt your situation looks different than David's in this psalm; however, we have much to learn from David's prayers to God in the midst of this crisis. According to scholar John Goldingay, Psalm 55 encourages those suffering . . .

- To throw onto God what God or other people throw onto us.
- To do this on behalf of churches in other parts of the world if we do not experience such attacks, as we enter into the trouble and harassment that they experience.
- To be open to God with the inner turmoil of our hearts and the outer turmoil that causes this.
- To be open with God about our longing to be away to the safety of some other place where we would not be subject to such experiences.
- To urge God to act directly to frustrate the plans of people who attack us.
- To draw God's attention to ways in which such malice characterizes the places where we live.
- To grieve before God at the way people who were members of our communities or our churches are the people who are now attacking us.
- To ask for God to deal justly with our attackers rather than taking matters into our own hands.
- To trust God to act justly on our behalf and to protect us.[19]

In the end, this psalm provides a very helpful expression of emotion and lament for anyone facing suffering, but especially those who have been harmed by someone who used to be a friend and trusted companion. David's emotions are deep and real. He is violently oppressed and he laments this fully, while expressing his aching hope for justice to be done to his enemy. He also calls out to God as the only one who really sees what is happening, asking Him to "hide not" and respond to rather than overlook this extreme injustice.

All this would be very applicable to someone experiencing physical abuse in a relationship. One commentator writes how this psalm may especially resonate with the experience of women who have suffered violence,

> which takes its most radical and painful form in rape, fundamentally not a sexual act but an act of violence that seeks to break and put down. As was the case with Tamar, this often involves someone the woman knows well, even someone within the family, and it often robs the woman of her speech (2 Sam. 13:20). The psalm can thus give her speech back. . . . This potential extends also to women subjected to other forms of sexual abuse, whom the psalm might help to express their pain and anger and to reach out to God for justice and healing.[20]

The injustice that has happened in this psalm is real, not imagined. This must be acknowledged and allowed to have full expression to move forward in a way that is appropriate and healthy.

And because the suffering is real, the perpetrator must be held accountable for this kind of violation. God has promised not to hide Himself forever. He sees it and will address it. But the psalm also shows that this may not happen the way we would like or expect, therefore our hope is always in God and His timing. He promises faithfulness as we trust and wait for Him.

The psalm begins with a despairing cry and ends with a statement of trust. The desperate singer, by the end of the psalm, turns his gaze away from the violence to look to God for a future ahead that does not end in suffering. This movement, from despair to trust, is encouraging and hopeful. The end of the psalm—"But I will trust in you"—is not a humiliating declaration of defeat at the hands of violence; rather, it is the discovery of an identity found in God—who is on the side of those suffering violence. Likewise, it is the letting go of an identity formed according to the violence perpetrated against him. Bail writes, "The ability to locate oneself in language, despite absolute powerlessness, can have a liberating effect, for it allows the silence about violence to be brought to an end so that the end of violence can begin."[21]

"But I will trust in you" is a call to God as an advocate of the afflicted, as their deliverer and refuge, and in so doing the afflicted gain strength to resist and are given back the identity that violence has stolen from them. The hope of finding a place of safety, hinted at in verses 4–8, is fulfilled and real as God is on the side of the victim and refuge for them. This trust in God is what makes it possible to name the action, to accuse perpetrators, and to hope for an end to the violence.

A Final Word

I f there is anything you take away from this book, we hope this is it: God knows and sees you in your experience of violence and abuse, He loves you through it all, and He greatly desires your safety and protection.

God has not forgotten you. He grieves with you. And we hope that knowing this will embolden you to be honest with both Him and others, and know that it is courageous—not shameful—to reach out for support.

Like David in these psalms, we hope you will not be silent or passive but express your emotions freely, cry, and grieve the pain and fear you have experienced. God has compassion for the victims of injustice, and at the root of His compassion is the fact that He witnesses the suffering of the abused. He sees your suffering, grieves with you in it, and longs for you to find freedom from it.

Affliction does not mean that God has forsaken His people. Rather, the constant biblical evidence is that God is on the move in response to prayers for deliverance. Not only that, but He equips us to move ourselves. The Psalms we have walked through show us that while David prayed to God for deliverance, he also took the necessary measures he needed to get to a safe place away from the violence. David prayed, but he also wisely fled and removed himself from the threat of violence.

While we cannot always observe this deliverance immediately, God will, no doubt, deliver His people. And in the meantime, we can wait actively—taking measures to get ourselves to a safe place where we can pursue the future God has called us to, a future that is hopeful, free, and healed of violence and abuse.

In a world where you have suffered from the one closest to you, the greatest promise we can offer is the assurance of God's loving and watchful presence. And He will give you the strength you need to do what's next.

As you discern what your next step is, remember that you have a voice and there are resources available to you. You don't have to remain silent anymore. Tell a friend, a family member, the authorities, a pastor, or ministry leader. You can find detailed practical ways to do this in appendix 2.

Jesus knows your sufferings. Jesus experienced violence at the hands of His own people. His identity was attacked. He was rejected and betrayed by others. He was abandoned. He was lied about, slandered, and personally attacked. He was humiliated. He was in emotional agony. He was in physical agony. He experienced the worst agony imaginable—not only physically on the cross but also emotionally and spiritually as well. At one point, He even cried out: "My God, my God, why have you forsaken me?" (Matt. 27:46).

Jesus endured the cross because of His compassion and love for you. He endured it so that you would be spared. The New Testament repeatedly turns to the cross of Christ as the supreme demonstration of the love of God (1 John 3:6; 4:8, 10). For the woman who feels forsaken by God, the sufferings of Jesus can be a great comfort. It is a comfort that exceeds the sympathy and comfort extended by others who have endured similar experiences. The God who embraces her is One who understands perfectly, grieves deeply, and loves completely.

There is hope. Rather than being simply a desire for a particular outcome that is uncertain, hope is characterized by certainty in the Bible. Hope is sure because God is behind the promise, and He has provided faithfully in the past to His people. The hope you need right now borrows from God's faithfulness in the past and anticipation of it in the future.

The basis you have for hope is the resurrection of Jesus from the dead. Christ's resurrection is a guarantee of your future resurrection to eternal life. Because of Jesus' resurrection, all threats against you are tamed if you trust in Christ. Jesus conquered death and evil, so death and evil done to you is not the end of the story and you can have hope. Because of the resurrection, your eyes can be fixed forward on the new creation, something wholly different—and better than broken life in the here and now.

You can also have hope now, not just in the future. Because God's plan for you is so certain, you can face the worst difficulties, the most terrifying enemies, and the most devastating ordeals with confidence. You do not merely survive your trials; you are sustained in the midst of them because absolutely nothing will be able to separate you from the love of God in Christ.

This all-loving God says to you clearly, it is *not* your fault. You were made for more than this. And it is His great desire to see you safe, healed, and made whole.

As you claim these truths in your own life and determine your next steps, this is our prayer for you borrowed from the *Book of Common Prayer*:

Comfort and heal all those who suffer in body, mind, or spirit; give them courage and hope in their trouble, and bring them the joy of your salvation.[1]

Acknowledgments

First of all, for those who have helped in many ways, we would like to thank Natalie Collins, Jeffrey Haines, Jordan Buckley, and Matt Johnson for their wisdom in helping us fine-tune this book.

At Moody, we would like to thank Holly Kisly and Stephanie Smith, and the rest of the team who supported the book marvelously.

Much gratitude for our researchers and editors from the Docent Research Group: Robert Velarde, James Gordon, Brad Vermurlen, and Andrew Hassler.

Finally, our sincere thanks go to all the brave victims who have trusted us with their stories of the violence they experienced and the healing they received and are still receiving from God. Your questions, insights, grief, affliction, hope, and healing have shaped every page of the book.

Getting Help

National Domestic Violence Hotline	1-800-799-7233 (SAFE)
	1-800-787-3224 (TTY)
National Domestic Violence Email	ndvh@ndvh.org
National Sexual Assault Hotline	1-800-656-4673
National Teen Dating Abuse Hotline	1-866-331-9474
National Child Abuse Hotline	1-800-222-4453

Appendix 2

Making a Safety Plan[1]

I f you are experiencing physical, sexual, emotional, and/or verbal abuse from a partner, spouse, family member, etc., you can create a personalized safety plan.

A personalized safety plan will help you know what to do if/when you decide to leave or find yourself (and children) in an emergency.

You can create this safety plan even if you are not ready to leave.

There are some important things that need to be considered. Evidence shows that planning before leaving is really important and is more likely to help the women stay away.

Please ensure that safety is considered when creating, printing, and/or completing this document. Considering who will have access to it and where it will be stored are extremely important.

SAFETY DURING A VIOLENT INCIDENT

In order to increase safety during a violent incident, you may use a variety of strategies. Here are some strategies for you to consider.

I can use the following options:

1. What are the possible escape route(s) from my home? What doors, windows, elevators, stairwells, or fire escapes could I use? I will take the time to practice how to get out safely.

   _____

2. I can keep my purse/wallet and keys handy, and always keep them in the same place (_____), so that I can

locate them easily if I need to leave in a hurry. I can also have a
second set of keys made in case my partner/ex takes the first set.

3. I can keep a bag ready and put it_____
   so I can leave quickly.

4. If it is safe for me, I could tell the following people about the violence and request that they call the police if they suspect I am
   in danger: _____ and

   _____

5. Children's safety in abuse situations is central to a safety plan. I
   may be able to teach my children a safety plan specifically for them
   in these circumstances. I can teach my children to use the telephone to call the police and the fire department.

6. It may be helpful to have a code word to use with my children,
   other family members, or friends if I should need them to call for
   help. I will use this word code: _____

   _____.

7. Safe places that I can go if I need to leave my home. Be pre-
   pared even if you think you will never have to leave.
   - A place to use the phone: _____

     _____
   - A place I could stay for a couple of hours:_____

     _____
   - A place that I could stay for a couple of days:_____

     _____
   - I can teach these strategies to my children.

8. When an abusive incidence occurs, I will move to a safer room.
   During an abusive incident, it is best to try to avoid places in the

house where I may be trapped or where weapons are readily available such as the bathroom or kitchen. Bigger rooms with more than one exit may be safer.

9. The places I would try to avoid would be: _____

_____

10. The places I would try to move to/stay in are: _____

_____

11. In abusive situations, women sometimes say or do things that in an equal non-abusive relationship they would not. For some women this involves survival skills such as claiming to agree with the abuser even when it's not true in order to increase safety. On other occasions, women may retaliate against the abuser with violence; however, be aware that such actions could lead you to be charged with a criminal offense.

12. Calling the police.

13. Given my past experience, other protective actions that I have considered or employed are: _____

_____

_____

_____

SAFETY PLANNING IF YOU ARE GETTING READY TO LEAVE

Some women leave the residence they share with the abusive partner. These are protective actions you may wish to consider if you are in this situation. Even if you are not planning to leave your partner, it is important to review a safety plan regarding leaving in case the violence escalates and you need to leave quickly.

I can use the following strategies:

1. It may not be safe to inform my partner that I am leaving.

2. Should I need to leave quickly, it would be helpful for me to leave some extra cash, an extra set of house and car keys and extra clothes with some people who I can go to for help:
   _____ and
   _____

3. I can keep copies of important documents such as immigration papers or birth certificates at someone's house: _____
   _____

4. I can open a savings account to increase my freedom to leave. I should make sure to alert the bank not to send any correspondence to my home address.

5. Other things I can do to increase my independence are: _____
   _____.

6. The domestic violence hotline is _____.
   I can seek safe shelter and support by calling this help line.

7. Telephone numbers I need to know:
   For safety reasons it may be necessary to keep these telephone numbers hidden but accessible!) and/or memorize the numbers:
   Police Department: _____
   _____
   Domestic Abuse Help Line (24 hours): _____
   _____
   Solicitor: _____
   _____

Work: _____

_____

Religious Leader (Minister/Rabbi/Priest/Imam): _____
Other: _____

_____

8. I can get legal advice from a victim advocate who understands domestic abuse. But as with the bank, I should make certain the advocate knows not to send any correspondence to my home address. It is critical to consult with a family advocate if you have children. Your local domestic abuse service may be able to recommend a suitable legal advocate.

9. I must be careful if I am using my mobile or home number because my partner or ex could see the numbers I have called on next month's telephone bill. I can keep telephone calls confidential by using a pay phone, a prepaid phone card, pay-as-you-go mobile phone, a friend's telephone card, or calling collect.

10. These are people that I could ask for assistance with:
Money: _____

_____

Child care: _____

_____

Support-attending appointments: _____

_____

Transportation: _____

_____

Other: _____

_____

11. If I need to return home to get personal belongings, I can call the police for an escort to stand by and keep the peace. To do this, I call _____ (the nonemergency local police number) and ask the police to meet me somewhere close to my home. They will stay while I pick up my own and my children's personal belongings.

12. I will review my safety plan every _____(time frame) in order to plan the safest route. I will review the plan with _____ (a friend, counselor, or advocate).

13. I will rehearse the escape plan and practice it with my children.

14. When you leave an abusive partner, it is important to take certain items with you. Items with asterisks on the following list are the most important, but if there is time, the other items might be taken, or stored outside the home. Keeping them all together in one location makes it much easier if you need to leave in a hurry.
Identification for myself
Children's birth certificates*
Any papers relating to injunctions or other legal proceedings*
My birth certificate*
Immigration papers*
School and vaccination records*
Money*
Checkbook, bankbook/cards*
Credit cards*
Keys—house/car/office*
Driver's license and car ownership details*
Medications*
Passport(s)*
Any medical records*
Divorce/separation papers*

House lease/mortgage/insurance documents*
Address book*
Pictures/photos
Children's favorite toys/blankets
Jewelry
Items of special sentimental value

15. Other protective actions I have considered are:

_____

_____

_____

SAFETY IN YOUR OWN HOME

The following are some suggestions regarding safety measures in your own home that you may wish to consider (some of these safety measures cost money).

I can use the following safety methods:

1. If financially possible, I could:
   - Change the locks on my doors and windows as soon as possible. (You may need to inform the landlord if you are renting or legal advocate if you own your home before taking this action.)
   - Install a peephole in the door.
   - Replace wooden doors with steel doors.
   - Install security systems—i.e., additional locks, window bars, poles to wedge against doors, electronic alarm system, etc.
   - Purchase rope ladders to be used for escape routes from the second floor.
   - Install smoke detectors and buy fire extinguishers for each floor of my home.

- Install a motion sensitive lighting system outside that lights up when a person is coming close to my home.
- Leave the lights on at night and when I am away from home.

2. If I have custody, I can inform all the people who provide child care for my children about who has permission to pick up my children and who does not. I can give these people copies of the custody order to keep with them and a picture of the abusive partner. I will tell the people who care for my children, who have permission to pick up my children. The people I will inform about pickup permission include:

School_____
Teacher_____
Nursery/Day Care staff_____
Before/After-School care_____
Babysitter_____
Sunday School_____
Relatives_____
Others_____

3. I can teach my children how to use the phone to make collect calls to me and to _____ (friend, family, minister) if my partner tries to take them.

4. I can tell my the following people that my partner no longer lives with me and ask that they should call the police if he is seen near my residence:

Neighbors_____
Landlord_____
Church Leaders_____
Friends_____

Others_____

5. Other strategies that I am already using or that I might use include:

_____

_____

_____

_____

SAFETY AT WORK AND IN PUBLIC

Each woman must decide if and/or when she will tell others that her partner has abused her and that she may be at continued risk. Friends, family, and coworkers may be able to help protect women. Each woman should consider carefully which people to recruit to help secure her safety. I might do any or all of the following:

1. If it is comfortable to do so, I can tell my boss, security, and _____ at work about this situation.

2. According to how comfortable and safe I feel, I can ask_____ _____ to help screen my phone calls.

3. If it is comfortable to do so, and I feel it would be supportive to me and my situation, I could discuss the possibility of having my employer call the police if I am in danger from my partner or ex.

4. Some safety suggestions regarding arriving or leaving work:
   - Let someone know when you'll be home
   - Walk with someone to your car
   - Scan the parking lot
   - If your partner is following you, drive to a place where there are people to support you, e.g., a friend's home, police station
   - If you are walking, take a route that is populated
   - Take different routes home

- If you see your partner on the street, try to get to a public place
- You can also call attention to yourself and request help
- Purchase a personal alarm device

5. When I am driving home from work and problems arise, I can

_____

6. I can use different supermarkets/shopping centers and shop at different times than I did before to reduce the risk of contact with my partner or ex.

SAFETY AND DRUG OR ALCOHOL CONSUMPTION

Alcohol and/or drugs are sometimes used as coping mechanisms for victims of domestic violence. The disclosure of the use of illegal/legal drugs can put a woman at a disadvantage in legal actions with her abusive partner. Therefore, women should carefully consider the potential cost of the use of legal and/or illegal drugs. Beyond this, the use of any alcohol or other drugs can reduce a woman's awareness and ability to act quickly to protect herself from the abusive partner. Furthermore, the use of alcohol or other drugs by the abuser may be used as an excuse for violence.

SAFETY AND EMOTIONAL HEALTH

Being subjected to abuse by partners is usually exhausting and emotionally draining. The process of surviving requires much courage and incredible energy. To conserve my emotional energy and resources and to support myself in hard emotional times, I can do some of the following:

1. If I have left the relationship and I am experiencing loneliness or manipulative tactics from my abusive partner, I can take care of myself by: _____

2. If I feel sad, lonely, or depressed and desire to return to a potentially violent situation/partner, I can_____ _____ and I can call _____

3. When I have to talk to my partner in person or on the phone, I can emotionally prepare by _____ _____

4. I can remind myself "_____ _____" if I feel people are trying to control or abuse me.

5. When I face potentially difficult times like court cases, meetings with lawyers, and such, I can prepare by doing the following_____ _____ _____ _____

6. I can call the following people and/or places for support: _____ _____ _____

7. Things I can do to make me feel stronger are _____ _____

8. I can find out about and attend workshops and support groups in the community by calling my local domestic abuse service on: _____ _____

Appendix 3

The Church and Women at Risk

W e've covered a lot of the material here in the main body of the book, but here's a quick summary of the theology and several practical tips for ministry staff in dealing with cases of domestic abuse.

The Bible teaches us that because of sin, suffering and violence entered the world. One expression of sin, which is seen throughout Scripture and human history, is violence against women. Even today, women around the world continue to experience violence and oppression in numerous forms: sexual assault, domestic violence, human trafficking, rape in warfare, female genital mutilation, infanticide, child marriages, girl soldiers, and honor killings.

Since the fall of humankind, women have often been oppressed, marginalized, and abused. Because life can be tragic for women, a biblical understanding of how the church can respond to women at risk is very important. Violence against women is a global health epidemic that affects women and girls of all socioeconomic backgrounds, ages, religions, cultures, races, and sexual orientations. Women and girls living in poverty and girls younger than eighteen are most vulnerable to the risk of violence.

THE BREAKING OF *SHALOM*

Violence and abuse toward women is a sin against the victims and a sin against God. When someone defaces a human being—God's image bearer—it is ultimately an attack against God Himself.

Genesis 3 records the terrible day when humanity fell into sin and *shalom* (the original peace of creation) was violated. This was a moment of cosmic treason, when Adam and Eve violated their relationship with God by rebelling against His command and fell under the curse of sin and bondage to corruption (Rom. 8:21) that we all experience.

The entrance of sin wrecked the order and goodness of God's world; it was the disintegration of peace. Sin inverted love for God, which in turn became idolatry, and inverted love for neighbor, which became exploitation of others.

THE BIBLICAL CALL TO JUSTICE AND MERCY

The Bible does not hesitate to depict the harsh reality of violence and oppression, and it clearly calls us to fight for justice and mercy for all people as God intended.

The prophet Zechariah portrays a God-given role for God's people as a nation that practices justice in their society: "Administer true justice; show mercy and compassion to one another. Do not oppress the widow or the fatherless, the foreigner or the poor. Do not plot evil against each other" (Zech 7:9–10). When Israel failed and continued to rebel against God's law, God threatened judgment, but then poured out grace and restored them. Zechariah envisions God's grace leading to true repentance and a people who fervently pursue justice and mercy. The result is that the nations of unbelievers will come asking about the Lord (Zech. 8:20–23). If God's people are thankful, worshiping God, and working for justice and mercy, it will make them a light to the nations (Isa. 49:6)—a hope that culminates in the coming of the Messiah.

JESUS' HEART FOR THE POWERLESS

At the beginning of Jesus' ministry, He stood up in the synagogue at Nazareth and declared that these words of Isaiah were fulfilled in Him:

> "The Spirit of the Lord is on me,
>   because he has anointed me

to proclaim good news to the poor.
He has sent me to proclaim freedom for the prisoners
   and recovery of sight for the blind,
to set the oppressed free,
to proclaim the year of the Lord's favor." (Luke 4:18–19)

In making this declaration and in His ministry, Jesus showed that bringing freedom for captives and relief to the poor and oppressed is at the very center of His divine mission. His ultimate act of liberation was His substitutionary death and victorious resurrection, which set His people free from slavery to sin and death. Yet His teachings and His example show us that the proclamation of the good news of Christ's saving work should be accompanied by tangible acts of love, service, and mercy toward our neighbors if the gospel message is to be recognized in its full power.

THE CHURCH'S OPPORTUNITY TO SERVE

The Christian church has, at its best, been known for exemplary love and sacrificial service to "the least of these"—the poor, oppressed, and marginalized. Such service has provided a powerful apologetic for the gospel. By upholding the dignity of all human life as the image of God and tangibly expressing the biblical ethic of personhood that flows from it, the church has the opportunity to be a light to the nations by welcoming the weak and powerless to find grace, mercy, and rest in Jesus Christ.

Unfortunately, many victims who reach out to churches in times of need receive blame, disbelief, suspicious questions, bad advice, platitudes, and shallow theology instead of care and compassion. Rather than pat answers, victims need practical victim advocacy full of biblical and theological depth.

Churches have a great opportunity to offer victims of violence love, safety, patience, and counseling. Caring for and responding to women at risk is an opportunity for Christians to take the gospel to those who are most in need, provide an alternative community centered on Jesus to the marginalized and oppressed, and show the transformative power of the gospel to the watching world. Moreover, responding to the epidemic of violence against women is a way the church can follow the charge of James to practice "pure religion" (James 1:27) by caring for vulnerable women.

Here are eight ways your church can reflect Jesus' heart for women at risk:

1. Know that God cares for those at risk and hates violence. Throughout the Bible we see an unrelenting concern of God for those who are weak, powerless, and oppressed. The complement of God's care for the oppressed is His hatred of violence. "Violence" is one of the first words used to describe the decay of the world after sin entered into it (Gen. 6:11–12). The Bible contains many examples of God's displeasure with violence, as well as the way God saves His people from it (see Ps. 11:5; Prov. 21:7; Zeph. 1:9; Mal. 2:16; Ps. 18:48; Isa. 60:18).

2. Stand with the vulnerable and powerless. God calls His people to resist those who use their power to oppress and harm others (Jer. 22:3).

3. Believe the women; don't blame them. Blaming victims for post-traumatic symptoms is not only erroneous but also contributes to the vicious cycle of traumatization, because victims who experience negative social reactions have poorer adjustment. Research has proven that being believed and being listened to by others are crucial to victims' healing.

4. Respond graciously, offering comfort, encouragement, and protection. Also respond with tangible, practical care. Spiritual and emotional support needs to be accompanied by actual deeds.

5. Get informed and inform others about the prevalence of women at risk. They can be found not only around the world but also right under our noses, in our cities and neighborhoods, and in our churches and small groups. The prevalence is staggering.

6. Learn about the effects of sexual assault, domestic violence, and other forms of abuse. The only thing more staggering than the prevalence of abuse toward women is the acute damage done to them. Trauma is not only *done to* but also *experienced by* victims. The internal and deeply personal places of a victim's heart, will, and emotions need a clear application of the gospel of redemption, along with tangible expressions of love.

7. Clearly communicate the hope and healing for victims that is found in the person and work of Jesus Christ. Unfortunately, the message victims hear most often is self-heal, self-love, and self-help. The church's message is not self-help but the grace of God. Grace does not command "Heal thyself!" but declares "You will be healed!" God's one-way love replaces self-love and is the true path to healing.

8. Get involved with the issue of violence against women. This can include addressing the issue in sermons, praying about it in corporate prayer, and working toward the prevention of abuse together with community and national organizations.

As we react to the pain and suffering of women at risk, we should meditate on Jesus' love and care for women. But God's love should do more than just make us feel better—it should lead us to imitate His care for children, take action against evil toward the vulnerable, and pray for God's peace and salvation to cover the earth.

PRAYER

"Almighty God, who created us in your image: Grant us grace fearlessly to contend against evil and to make no peace with oppression; and, that we may reverently use our freedom, help us to employ it in the maintenance of justice in our communities and among the nations, to the glory of your holy Name; through Jesus Christ our Lord, who lives and reigns with you and the Holy Spirit, one God, now and for ever. *Amen.*"[1]

Recommended Reading[1] and Bibliography[2]

CHRISTIAN RESOURCES

Adams, Carol J. *Woman Battering.* Philadelphia: Fortress, 1994.

This is an excellent resource on domestic violence for clergy. It is very practical, readable, and covers a wide variety of issues.

Alsdurf, James, and Phyllis Alsdurf. *Battered into Submission: The Tragedy of Wife Abuse in the Christian Home.* Downers Grove, IL: InterVarsity, 1989.

This is a landmark study of domestic violence in the church.

Kroeger, Catherine Clark, and Nancy Nason-Clark. *No Place for Abuse: Biblical and Practical Resources to Counteract Domestic Violence.* Downers Grove, IL: InterVarsity, 2001.

This is also an excellent practical resource for churches and domestic violence victims.

_____. *Refuge from Abuse: Healing and Hope for Abused Christian Women.* Downers Grove, IL: InterVarsity, 2004.

This is a practical guide to help abused Christian women heal.

Livingston, David. *Healing Violent Men: A Model for Christian Community.* Minneapolis: Fortress, 2002.

This is one of the few books on how the church should relate and minister to batterers.

Miles, Al. *Domestic Violence: What Every Pastor Needs to Know.* Philadelphia: Fortress, 2000.

This is one of the best books in print for clergy on domestic violence.

Nason-Clark, Nancy. *The Battered Wife: How Christians Confront Family Violence.* Louisville: Westminster/John Knox, 1997.

This is a thoroughly researched work by one of the most respected Christian domestic violence scholars.

Tracy, Steven. *Mending the Soul: Understanding and Healing Abuse.* Grand Rapids: Zondervan, 2005.

This is a comprehensive, practical treatment of all forms of abuse, including domestic violence. It integrates biblical, theological principles with social science research.

————. "Clergy Responses to Domestic Violence," *Priscilla Papers,* 21:2 (spring 2007): 9–16.

This is a short but comprehensive guide to clergy responses to domestic violence.

SECULAR RESOURCES

Bancroft, Lundy. *Why Does He Do That? Inside the Minds of Angry and Controlling Men.* New York: G. P. Putnam's Sons, 2002.

This is a very thorough but nontechnical overview of abusive men. It also has a very helpful section on helping abusers change.

Dutton, Donald G. *The Batterer: A Psychological Profile.* New York: Basic Books, 1995.

Dutton is one of the country's leading experts on batterers. This is an excellent psychological treatment of the characteristics of batterers.

Gelles, Richard J. *Intimate Violence in Families.* 3rd ed. Thousand Oaks, CA: Sage, 1997.

This is one of the best readable overviews of family violence by one of the most respected psychological experts in the field.

Jacobson, Neil, and John Gottman. *When Men Batter Women: New Insights into Ending Abusive Relationships.* New York: Simon & Shuster, 1998.

This book offers a practical summary of a landmark study on violent relationships conducted by two of the countries leading psychological experts.

Walker, Lenore. *The Battered Woman.* New York: Harper & Row, 1979.

This is one of the classic treatments on domestic violence. It is very readable and insightful, particularly Walker's three-phase model of the abuse cycle.

NOTES

Foreword

1. http://domesticviolencestatistics.org/domestic-violence-statistics/.
2. Ibid.

Introduction

1. Patricia Tjaden and Nancy Thoennes, "Extent, Nature and Consequences of Intimate Partner Violence: Findings from the National Violence Against Women Survey" (2000). National Institute of Justice and the Centers for Disease Control and Prevention.

2. J. Gordon, "Community Services Available to Abused Women in Crisis: A Review of Perceived Usefulness and Efficacy," *Journal of Family Violence* (1996): 11:4; 315–29. Gordon's study examined twelve outcomes studies on the effectiveness of intervention by community social services, crisis hotlines, women's groups, police, clergy, physicians, psychotherapists, and lawyers. Abused women consistently found crisis hotlines, women's groups, social workers, and psychotherapists to be very helpful. In sharp contrast, the abused women reported that usually police, clergy, and lawyers were not helpful.

3. Justin S. Holcomb, *On the Grace of God* (Wheaton: Crossway, 2013), 11–12.

Chapter 1: Deliver Us from Evil

1. Lundy Bancroft, *Why Does He Do That? Inside the Minds of Angry and Controlling Men* (New York: G. P. Putnam's Sons, 2002), 352.

2. Hans Boersma, *Violence, Hospitality, and the Cross: Reappropriating the Atonement Tradition* (Grand Rapids: Baker Academic, 2006), 44.

3. Wolfgang Huber, *Violence: The Unrelenting Assault on Human Dignity*, trans. Ruth C. L. Gritsch (Minneapolis: Fortress, 1996), 128.

4. Donald X. Burt, *Friendship and Society: An Introduction to Augustine's Practical Philosophy* (Grand Rapids: Eerdmans, 1999), 162.

5. Leo D. Lefebure, *Revelation, the Religions, and Violence* (Maryknoll, NY: Orbis Books, 2000), 13.

6. Diane Langberg, *Counseling Survivors of Sexual Abuse* (Maitland, FL: Xulon Press, 2003), 29.

7. Ron Clark, *Setting the Captives Free* (Eugene, OR: Cascade, 2005), xxi. As Clark puts it, "Domestic violence is not only a crime against humanity, it is a sin against God. The community of faith is called to protect victims and prevent the abuse of power. 'Open your mouth for those who cannot speak to bring justice to the weak. Open your mouth and judge righteously, and bring justice to the oppressed and poor' (Proverbs 31:8–9). The faith community is called to represent God and call men and women to love, compassion, gentleness, and respect for themselves and each other. The community of faith must deal with domestic violence because it has penetrated our families, our neighborhoods, our com-

munity, our churches, and our world. Domestic violence crosses all racial, ethnic, cultural, social, and gender boundaries and is destroying families, children, businesses, friends, and the structure of our society. Yet a greater crime exists. It is the crime of apathy and silence. To ignore this violence and humiliation is to ignore the voice of God. To pat the victims on the head and minimize their pain is to slap God in the face. To go to our homes and sleep at night, without being compelled to act, while others live in terror and fear is ignoring our duty to God and our neighbor."

Chapter 2: Am I in an Abusive Relationship?

1. The Freedom Progamme: www.freedomprogramme.co.uk.

2. Some abusers may even use Scripture against their victim by misusing verses such as 1 Corinthians 7:5: "Do not deprive one another, except perhaps by agreement for a limited time, that you may devote yourselves to prayer; but then come together again, so that Satan may not tempt you because of your lack of self-control." Some wrongly conclude that this verse connotes that the spouse owes her husband by giving her body to him whenever he pleases. But this reading misses that the marriage bed is about giving to one another willingly, rather than through coercion.

3. http://www.helpguide.org/mental/domestic_violence_abuse_types_signs_causes_effects.htm.

4. Justin S. Holcomb and Lindsey A. Holcomb, *Rid of My Disgrace: Hope and Healing for Victims of Sexual Assault* (Wheaton: Crossway, 2011), 28.

5. Ruth E. Hall, *Ask Any Woman: A London Inquiry into Rape and Sexual Assault* (London: Falling Wall, 1985); M. Koss, C. A. Gidycz, and N. Wisniewski, "The Scope of Rape: Incidence and Prevalence of Sexual Aggression and Victimization in a National Sample of Higher Education Students," *Journal of Consulting and Clinical Psychology* 55 (1987): 162–70; M. Koss, "Rape: Scope, Impact, Interventions, and Public Policy Responses," *American Psychologist* 48 (1993): 1062–69; D. G. Kilpatrick et al., "Criminal Victimization: Lifetime Prevalence, Reporting to Police, and Psychological Impact," *Crime and Delinquency* 33 (1987): 479–89; D. G. Kilpatrick and A. Seymour, "Rape in America: A Report to the Nation" (National Victims Center: Arlington, VA, and Crime Victims Research and Treatment Center: Charleston, SC, 1992); M. Koss and T. E. Dinero, "Discrimination Analysis of Risk Factors for Sexual Victimization among a National Sample of College Women," *Journal of Consulting and Clinical Psychology* 57 (1989): 242–50; P. Tjaden and N. Thoennes, "Prevalence, Incidence, and Consequences of Violence Against Women: Findings from the National Violence Against Women Survey" (Washington, D.C.: U.S. Department of Justice, 1998); and S. B. Sorenson et al., "The Prevalence of Adult Sexual Assault: The Los Angeles Epidemiologic Catchment Area Project," *American Journal of Epidemiology* 126 (1987): 1154–64. An estimated 20–25 percent of college women in the United States experience attempted or completed rape during their college careers (B. S. Fisher, F. T. Cullen, M. G. Turner, "The Sexual Victimization of College Women" [Washington, D.C.: Department of Justice, National Institute of Justice, 2000]). On college campuses, 74 percent of victims knew their assailant and nine out of ten offenders included boyfriends,

ex-boyfriends, classmates, friends, and acquaintances (Timothy Hart, "Violent Victimization of College Students" [U.S. Department of Justice: Office of Justice Programs, Bureau of Justice Statistics Special Report: 2003] http://bjs.ojp.usdoj. gov/ index.cfm?ty=pbdetail&iid=496).

6. R. K. Bergen, *Wife Rape: Understanding the Response of Survivors and Service Providers* (Thousand Oaks, CA: Sage, 1996); D. G. Finkelhor and K. Yllo, *License to Rape: Sexual Abuse of Wives* (New York: Holt, Rinehart, and Winston, 1985); D. E. H. Russell, *Rape in Marriage* (Indianapolis: Indiana University Press, 1990); P. Mahoney and L. Williams, "Sexual Assault in Marriage: Prevalence, Consequences and Treatment for Wife Rape," in *Partner Violence: A Comprehensive Review of 20 Years of Research*, ed. J. L. Jasinski and L. M. Williams (Thousand Oaks, CA: Sage, 1998).

7. *Breaking the Silence: A Handbook for Victims of Violence in Nebraska*, http://lancaster.ne.gov/attorney/pdf/silence.pdf.

8. Ann Jones and Susan Schecter, *When Loves Goes Wrong: What to Do When You Can't Do Anything Right. Strategies for Women with Controlling Partners* (New York: HarperCollins, 1992), 13.

9. In 1984, staff at the Domestic Abuse Intervention Project (DAIP) began developing curricula for groups for men who batter and victims of domestic violence. http://www.theduluthmodel.org/training/wheels.html.

10. Anne L. Ganley, *Court Mandated Counseling for Men Who Batter: A Three-Day Workshop for Mental Health Professionals* (Washington, D.C.: Center for Women Policy Studies, 1981), 9.

11. Lenore Walker, *The Battered Woman Syndrome* (New York: Springer Publishing, 1984).

12. http://www.helpguide.org/mental/domestic_violence_abuse_types_signs_causes_effects.htm.

13. Lundy Bancroft, *Why Does He Do That? Inside the Minds of Angry and Controlling Men* (New York: G. P. Putnam's Sons, 2002), 75.

Chapter 3: Why Does He Choose to Abuse?

1. Neil Jacobson and John Gottman, *When Men Batter Women: New Insights into Ending Abusive Relationships* (New York: Simon & Schuster, 1998), 183.

2. Steven Tracy writes, "The etiology of domestic violence is quite complex, most likely involving biological (differences in brain structure, brain functioning, and hormones), intrapsychic (personality and attachment disorders), and social construct (childhood experiences of violence) factors in men's violence against women." See "Clergy Responses to Domestic Violence," *Priscilla Papers* 21:2 (spring 2007): 9–16. Two of the most thorough discussions of the complex factors behind male-perpetrated domestic violence are Michele Harway and James M. O'Neil, eds., *What Causes Men's Violence Against Women?* (Thousand Oaks, CA: Sage, 1999) and Karel Kurst-Swanger and Jacqueline L. Petcosky, *Violence in the Home: Multidisciplinary Perspectives* (Oxford: Oxford University Press, 2003), 30–53.

3. Most of what follows is from Catherine Clark Kroeger and Nancy Nason-Clark, *No Place for Abuse* (Downers Grove, IL: InterVarsity, 2001), 57–59 and Helen L. Conway, *Domestic Violence and the Church* (Milton Keynes, UK: Paternoster, 1998), 25–28.

4. Calgary Women's Emergency Shelter (2007). *Honouring Resistance: How Women Resist Abuse in Intimate Relationships*, 3 (formerly *Resistance to Violence and Abuse in Intimate Relationships: A Response-Based Perspective*). Available from Calgary Women's Emergency Shelter, P.O. Box 52051 Edmonton Trail N., Calgary, Alberta T2E 8K9.

Chapter 4: What Is Domestic Violence?

1. Instead of "domestic violence" it could be more accurately termed "intimate partner abuse" for two reasons. First, "domestic" implies that the violence takes place in the home. Whereas, the violence can take place anywhere, and the partners do not need to be living together for there to be an abusive relationship. Second, for most people "violence" usually means only physical abuse, but there are other types of abuse commonly employed by abusers: sexual abuse, emotional abuse, and financial abuse. For these reasons, the term "intimate partner abuse" is a more inclusive and accurate term.

2. The Council of Europe "Convention on Preventing and Combating Violence Against Women and Domestic Violence" states that: "'domestic violence' shall mean all acts of physical, sexual, psychological or economic violence that occur within the family or domestic unit or between former or current spouses or partners, whether or not the perpetrator shares or has shared the same residence with the victim" (http://conventions.coe.int/Treaty/EN/Treaties/Html/210. htm). Article 2 of the UN "Declaration on the Elimination of Violence Against Women" classifies violence against women into three categories: that occurring in the family, that occurring within the general community, and that perpetrated or condoned by the State. Family violence is defined as follows: "Physical, sexual and psychological violence occurring in the family, including battering, sexual abuse of female children in the household, dowry-related violence, marital rape, female genital mutilation and other traditional practices harmful to women, non-spousal violence and violence related to exploitation" (http://www.un.org/ documents/ga/res/48/a48r104.htm). In Malta, the "Act XX on Domestic Violence 2006" defines domestic violence: "'Domestic violence' means any act of violence, even if only verbal, perpetrated by a household member upon another household member and includes any omission which causes physical or moral harm to the other" (http://sgdatabase.unwomen.org/uploads/Malta%20-%20 Act%20XX%20on%20domestic%20violence%20%28eng%29.pdf).

3. Laura I. O'Toole and Jessica R. Schiffman, eds., *Gender Violence Interdisciplinary Perspective* (New York: New York University Press, 1997), xii.

4. "Violence now includes such a phenomenologically elusive categories as psychological, symbolic, structural, epistemic, hermeneutical, and aesthetic violence." Beatrice Hanssen, *Critique of Violence: Between Poststructuralism and Critical Theory*, Warwick Studies in European Philosophy (New York: Routledge, 2000).

5. Examples of physical violence include kicks, punches, slaps, pushes, burns, use of weapons, pulling hair, shaking, dragging, choking, biting, etc.

6. Stalking means intentional, knowing or reckless, repeated and unwanted contact with the victim that causes the victim reasonable fear regarding physical safety. Over 8 percent of women have been stalked at some time in their life. Patricia Tjaden and Nancy Thoennes, "Full Report of the Prevalence, Incidence, and Consequences of Violence Against Women: Findings from the National Violence Against Women Survey" (Washington, D.C.: U.S. Department of Justice, National Institute of Justice, 2000).

7. Grace Ketterman writes that verbal abuse has seven different ingredients: "1. Verbal abuse causes emotional damage because of the victim's sense of rejection of his or her value as a person. 2. Verbal abuse may isolate its victim from social activities and friendships by destroying the self-esteem required for such relationships. 3. Verbal abuse creates terror in the victim. The fear that he or she is worthless destroys hope for the future. 4. Verbal abuse ignores the basic needs of its victims. Everyone has three basic emotional needs: unconditional acceptance, approval, and consistency. The victim of ongoing verbal abuse knows only the last of these, and then only in an emotionally damaging way. 5. Verbal abuse may corrupt the values and behaviors of the victim through the use of vulgar language and crude accusations. 6. Verbal abuse degrades victims by robbing them of self-esteem. 7. Verbal abuse exploits its victim for the benefits of the abuser, especially from a temporary sense of power—false as it is—unleashed during the abusive tirade." Grace Ketterman, *Verbal Abuse: Healing the Hidden Wound* (Ventura, CA: Vine Books, 1993), 12–13.

8. Abuse can also be economic, keeping the victims short of money or deliberately getting the family into debt. Some abusers humiliate victims by making them account for every penny they spend and criticizing their choices.

9. E. J. Alpert, S. Cohen, and R. D. Sege, "Family Violence: An Overview," *Academic Medicine* 72 (1997): S3–S6; P. A. Barrier, "Domestic Violence," *Mayo Clinic Proc.* 73 (1998): 271–74; M. T. Loring, and R. W. Smith, "Health Care Barriers and Interventions for Battered Women," *Public Health Reports* 109 (1994): 328–38; K. S. Moehling, "Battered Women and Abusive Partners: Treatment Issues and Strategies," *Journal of Psychosocial Nursing* 26 (1998): 9–16; R. L. Muelleman, P. A. Leneghan, and R. A. Pakieser, "Battered: Injury Locations and Types," *Annals of Emergency Medicine* 28 (1996): 486–92; R. L. Muelleman, J. Reuwer, T. G. Sanson et al., "An Emergency Medicine Approach to Violence throughout the Life Cycle," *Academic Emergency Medicine* 3 (1996): 708–15; A. C. Novello, "From the Surgeon General, U.S. Public Health Services: A Medical Response to Domestic Violence," *Journal of the American Medical Association* 267 (1992): 3132; L. E. Saltzman and D. Johnson, "CDC's Family and Intimate Violence Prevention Team: Basing Programs on Science," *Journal of the American Medical Women's Association* 51 (1996): 83–86; L. E. Saltzman, J. L. Fanslow, P. M. McMahon, and G. A. Shelley, *Intimate Partner Violence Surveillance: Uniform Definitions and Recommended Data Elements* (Atlanta: National Center for Injury Prevention and Control, Centers for Disease Control and Prevention, 1999).

10. Alpert, Cohen, and Sege, "Family Violence: An Overview;" J. C. Campbell and K. L. Soeke, "Women's Responses to Battering: A Test of the Model," *Research in Nursing and Health* 22 (1999): 49–58; K. Healey, C. Smith, and C. O'Sullivan, "Batterer Intervention: Program Approaches and Criminal Justice Strategies,"

Issues and Practices in Criminal Justice. National Institute of Justice [Online]. Available: http://www.ncjrs.org/txtfiles/168638.txt, 1998; Muelleman, Leneghan, and Pakieser, "Battered: Injury Locations and Types"; Muelleman, Reuwer, Sanson et al., "An Emergency Medicine Approach to Violence throughout the Life Cycle"; Saltzman and Johnson, "CDC's Family and Intimate Violence Prevention Team: Basing Programs on Science."

11. Campbell and Soeke, "Women's Responses to Battering"; Healey, Smith, and O'Sullivan, "Batterer Intervention"; Muelleman, Leneghan, and Pakieser, "Battered: Injury Locations and Types"; Muelleman, Reuwer, Sanson et al., "An Emergency Medicine Approach to Violence throughout the Life Cycle"; Saltzman and Johnson, "CDC's Family and Intimate Violence Prevention Team."

12. L. R. Chambliss, "Domestic Violence: A Public Health Crisis," *Clinical Obstetrics and Gynecology* 40 (1997): 630–38; Healey, Smith, and O'Sullivan, "Batterer Intervention"; L. E. Keller, "Invisible Victims: Battered Women in Psychiatric and Medical Emergency Rooms," *Bulletin of the Menninger Clinic* 60 (1996): 1–21; S. Y. Melvin and M. C. Rhyne, "Domestic Violence," *Advanced Internal Medicine* 43 (1998): 1–25; Muelleman, Leneghan, and Pakieser, "Battered: Injury Locations and Types"; Muelleman, Reuwer, Sanson et al., "An Emergency Medicine Approach to Violence throughout the Life Cycle."

13. Tjaden and Thoennes, "Extent, Nature and Consequences of Intimate Partner Violence: Findings from the National Violence Against Women Survey," National Institute of Justice and the Centers for Disease Control and Prevention, 2000; Tjaden and Thoennes, "Full Report of the Prevalence, Incidence, and Consequences of Violence Against Women Survey," Findings from the National Violence Against Women Survey. Research Report. Washington, D.C., and Atlanta: U.S. Department of Justice, National Institute of Justice, and U.S. Department of Health and Human Services, Centers for Disease Control and Prevention, November 2000, NCJ 183781; Sara Glazer, "Violence, Against Women," CO Researcher, *Congressional Quarterly* 3, no. 8 (February 1993): 171; The Commonwealth Fund, Health Concerns across a Woman's Life Span: 1998 Survey of Women's Health, 1999; U.S. Department of Justice, Violence by Intimates: Analysis of Data on Crimes by Current or Former Spouses, Boyfriends, and Girlfriends, 1988; N. S. Jecker, "Privacy Beliefs and the Violent Family: Extending the Ethical Argument for Physician Intervention," *Journal of the American Medical Association* 269 (1993): 776–80; Loring, and Smith, "Health Care Barriers and Interventions for Battered Women."

14. Campbell and Soeke, "Women's Responses to Battering"; D. Gaffigan-Bender and M. Narula, "Domestic Violence: Listening for the Truths That Patients Are Afraid to Tell," *Physical Therapy Magazine* (1998): 72–84; Keller, "Invisible Victims: Battered Women in Psychiatric and Medical Emergency Rooms," 1–21; Muelleman, Reuwer, Sanson et al., "An Emergency Medicine Approach to Violence throughout the Life Cycle"; Novello, "From the Surgeon General, U.S. Public Health Services: A Medical Response to Domestic Violence," 3132; Tjaden and Thoennes, "Full Report of the Prevalence, Incidence, and Consequences of Violence Against Women: Findings from the National Violence Against Women Survey." Tjaden and Thoennes, "Extent, Nature and Consequences of Intimate Partner Violence: Findings from the National Violence

Against Women Survey"; Bureau of Justice Statistics, Violence Against Women: Estimates from the Redesigned Survey, August 1995.

15. Ron Clark, *Setting the Captives Free: A Christian Theology for Domestic Violence* (Eugene, OR: Cascade, 2005), xx.

16. Allstate Foundation National Poll on Domestic Violence, 2006. Lieberman Research Inc., Tracking Survey conducted for the Advertising Council and the Family Violence Prevention Fund, July–October 1996.

17. Helen M. Eigengerg, *Women Battering in the United States: Till Death Do Us Part* (Prospect Heights, IL: Waveland Press, 2001), 62–85. One of the largest and most cited surveys of domestic violence is the "Violence Against Women Survey," which was a joint effort by the National Institute for Justice and the Centers for Disease Control. It involved a random sample survey of 8,000 men and 8,000 women. This survey found a lifetime intimate assault rate for American women of 22 percent (25 percent if sexual assaults are included); Tjaden and Thoennes, "Prevalence, Incidence, and Consequences of Violence Against Women: Findings from the National Violence Against Women Survey." Using a screening tool recommended by the American Medical Association, researchers in another study found a 31 percent lifetime prevalence for domestic violence among adult American women; R. M. Siegel et al., "Screening for Domestic Violence in a Community Pediatric Setting," *Pediatrics* 104 (1999): 874–77; M. C. Black, K. C. Basile, M. J. Breiding, S. G. Smith, M. L. Walters, M. T. Merrick, J. Chen, and M. R. Stevens (Atlanta: National Center for Injury Prevention and Control, Centers for Disease Control and Prevention, 2011); Center for Health and Gender Equity, Mental Health and Behavioural Outcomes of Sexual Abuse: Data Summary. Takoma (Park, MD: Center for Health and Gender Equity, 1999); C. Kershaw, N. Chivite-Matthews, C. Thomas, R. Aust, "The 2001 British Crime Survey," http://www.homeoffice.gov.uk/rds/pdfs/hosb1801.pdf; B. Spitzberg, "The Tactical Topography of Stalking Victimization and Management," *Trauma Violence Abuse* 3:4 (2002): 261–88; and Tjaden and Thoennes, "Extent, Nature and Consequences of Intimate Partner Violence: Findings from the National Violence Against Women Survey."

18. U.S. Department of Justice, Bureau of Justice Statistics, "Intimate Partner Violence in the United States," December 2006; U.S. Department of Justice, Bureau of Justice Statistics, "Criminal Victimization, 2005," September 2006.

19. U.S. Department of Justice, Bureau of Justice Statistics, "Criminal Victimization, 2005," September 2006.

20. Bureau of Justice Statistics Crime Data Brief, "Intimate Partner Violence," 1993–2001, February 2003.

21. Callie Marie Rennison and Sarah Welchans, "Intimate Partner Violence," U.S. Department of Justice: Bureau of Justice Statistics Special Report, May 2000.

22. Tjaden and Thoennes, "Extent, Nature and Consequences of Intimate Partner Violence: Findings from the National Violence Against Women Survey," National Institute of Justice and the Centers of Disease Control and Prevention, 2000.

23. See, for example, R. Bachman, "Violence Against Women: A National Crime Victimization Survey Report" (Washington, D.C.: U.S. Department of Justice, Bureau of Justice Statistics, 1994), NCJ 145325; R. Bachman and L. E.

Saltzman, "Violence Against Women: Estimates from the Redesigned Survey," Special Report (Washington, D.C.: U.S. Department of Justice, Bureau of Justice Statistics, 1995), NCJ 154348; R. A. Berk, S. F. Berk, D. R. Loseke, and D. Rauma, "Mutual Combat and Other Family Victim Myths," in *The Dark Side of Families*, ed. D. Finkelhor, D. O. Gelles, G. T. Hotaling, and M. A. Straus (Beverly Hills, CA: Sage, 1983), 197–212; M. Bograd, "Family Systems Approaches to Wife Battering: A Feminist Critique," *American Journal of Orthopsychiatry* 54 (1984): 558–68; R. E. Dobash and R. P. Dobash, "Wives: The Appropriate Victims of Marital Violence," *Victimology: An International Journal* 2 (3/4) (1977–78): 426–43; R. E. Dobash, R. P. Dobash, M. Wilson, and M. Daly, "The Myth of Sexual Symmetry in Marital Violence," *Social Problems* 39 (1992): 71–91; D. Kurz,, "Social Science Perspectives and Wife Abuse: Current Debates and Future Directions," *Gender and Society* 3 (1989): 501–13; D. Gaquin, "Spouse Abuse: Data from the National Crime Survey," *Victimology* 2 (1977–78): 634–43; L. Greenfeld, M. R. Rand, D. Craven, P. A. Klaus, C. A. Perkins, C. Ringel, G. Warchol, C. Matson, and J. A. Fox, "Violence by Intimates: Analysis of Data on Crimes by Current or Former Spouses, Boyfriends, and Girlfriends," Bureau of Justice Statistics Factbook (Washington, D.C.: U.S. Department of Justice, Bureau of Justice Statistics, 1998), NCJ 167237; P. Klaus and M. Rand, Family Violence, Special Report (Washington, D.C.: U.S. Department of Justice, Bureau of Justice Statistics, 1984), NCJ 093449. E. Pleck, J. H. Pleck, M. Grossman, and P. Bart, "The Battered Date Syndrome: A Comment on Steinmetz's Article," *Victimology* 4 (1977–78), 131–40; L. Wardell, D. L. Gillespie, and A. Leffler, "Science and Violence Against Wives," in *The Dark Side of Families*, ed. D. Finkelhor, R. J. Gelles, G. T. Hotaling, and M. A. Straus (Beverly Hills, CA: Sage, 1983), 69–84; Tjaden and Thoennes, "Extent, Nature, and Consequences of Intimate Partner Violence: Findings from the National Violence Against Women Survey."

24. U.S. Department of Justice, Bureau of Justice and Statistics, "Intimate Partner Violence in the United States, 1993–2004," December 2006.

25. Ibid.

26. Liz Claiborne, Inc., Omnibuzz Topline Findings: "Teen Relationship Abuse Research," available at www.teenresearch.com.

27. Tjaden and Thoennes, "Full Report of the Prevalence, Incidence, and Consequences of Violence Against Women: Findings from the National Violence Against Women Survey."

28. R. McDonald, "Estimating the Number of American Children Living in Partner Violent Families," *Journal of Family Psychology* 30:1 (2006): 137–42.

29. The landmark study that established this correlation was done by Murray Straus, and reported in "Ordinary Violence, Child Abuse, and Wife-Beating: What Do They Have in Common?" in *Physical Violence in American Families*, ed. Murray Straus and Richard Gelles (New Brunswick, NJ: Transition, 1990), 403–24.

30. Bruce Perry, "The Neurodevelopmental Impact of Violence in Childhood," in *Textbook of Child and Adolescent Forensic Psychiatry*, ed. D. Schetky and E. Benedek (Washington, D.C.: American Psychiatric Press, 2001), 21–38.

31. D. A. Wolfe, C. Wekerle, D. Reitzel, and R. Gough, "Strategies to Address Violence in the Lives of High Risk Youth," in *Ending the Cycle of Violence:*

Community Responses to Children of Battered Women, ed. E. Peled, P. G. Jaffe and J. L. Edleson (New York: Sage, 1995).

32. Inat Peled, Peter C. Jaffe, and Jeffrey L. Edleson, eds., *Ending the Cycle of Violence: Community Responses to Children of Battered Women* (Thousand Oaks, CA: Sage, 1995).

33. Carol J. Adams, *Woman Battering* (Philadelphia: Fortress, 1994), 21.

34. I. Frieze and A. Browne, "Violence in Marriage," in *Family Violence*, ed. L. Ohlin and M. Tonry (Chicago: University of Chicago Press, 1989), 163–68.

35. M. A. Straus and R. J. Gelles, *Physical Violence in American Families: Risk Factors and Adaptations to Violence in 8,145 Families* (Piscataway, NJ: Transaction Publishers, 1992).

36. C. L. Whitfield, R. F. Anda, S. R. Dube, and V. J. Felitti, "Violent Childhood Experiences and the Risk of Intimate Partner Violence in Adults," *Journal of Interpersonal Violence* 18 (2003): 166–85.

37. Adams, *Woman Battering*, 22.

38. Ibid.

39. Tjaden and Thoennes, "Extent, Nature, and Consequences of intimate Partner Violence: Findings from the National Violence Against Women Survey."

40. Ibid.

41. C. Humphreys and R. Thiara, *Routes to Safety: Protection issues facing abused women and children and the role of outreach services* (Women's Aid Federation of England: Bristol, 2002). This study of 200 women's experiences of domestic violence commissioned by Women's Aid, found that 60 percent of the women had left because they feared that they or their children would be killed by the perpetrator.

42. National Clearinghouse for the Defense of Battered Women (1994). Statistics packet (3rd ed.), Philadelphia.

43. K. Yllo and M. Straus, "Interpersonal Violence among Married and Cohabiting Couples," *Family Relations* 30 (1981): 339–47; J. E. Stets and M. A. Straus, "The Marriage License as a Hitting License: A Comparison of Assaults in Dating, Cohabiting, and Married Couples," *Journal of Family Violence* 4 (2) (1989): 161–80; L. Ellis, *Theories of Rape: Inquiries into the Causes of Sexual Aggression* (New York: Hemisphere Books), 1989.

44. For example, see Ronet Bachman, *Death and Violence on the Reservation: Homicide, Family Violence, and Suicide in American Indian Populations* (Westport, CT: Auburn House, 1992); N. A. Cazenave and M. A. Straus, "Race, Class, Network Embeddedness and Family Violence: A Search for Potent Support Systems," *Journal of Comparative Family Studies* 10 (3) (1979): 281–300; R. Gelles, "Violence in the Family: A Review of Research in the Seventies," *Journal of Marriage and the Family* 42 (1980): 873–85; R. L. Hampton, "Family Violence and Homicides in the Black Community: Are They Linked?" in *Violence in the Black Family: Correlates and Consequences*, ed. R. L. Hampton (Lexington, MA: 1987): 135–87; J. A. Neff, B. Holamon, and T. D. Schluter, "Spousal Violence among Anglos, Blacks, and Mexican Americans: The Role of Demographic Variables, Psychological Predictors, and Alcohol Consumption,"

Journal of Family Violence 10:1 (1995): 1–21; D. J. Shoemaker and J. S. Williams, "The Subculture of Violence and Ethnicity," *Journal of Criminal Justice* 15:6 (1987): 461–72; and M. A. Straus, R. J. Gelles, and S. Steinmetz, eds., *Behind Closed Doors* (Newbury Park, CA: Sage, 1980).

45. R. Bachman, *Violence Against Women*; R. Bachman and L. E. Saltzman, "Violence Against Women: Estimates From the Redesigned Survey," Special Report (Washington, D.C.: U.S. Department of Justice, Bureau of Justice Statistics, 1995), NCJ 154348; Straus, Gelles, and Steinmetz, eds., *Behind Closed Doors* (Newbury Park, CA: Sage, 1980); M. W. Zawit, "Violence between Intimates," (Washington, D.C.: U.S. Department of Justice, Bureau of Justice Statistics, 1994), NCJ 149259.

46. Bachman and Saltzman, "Violence Against Women, Estimates from the Redesigned Survey"; Zawit, "Violence Between Intimates," 1994, NCJ 149259; C. A. Hornung, B. C. McCullough, and T. Sugimoto, "Status Relationships in Marriage, Risk Factors in Spouse Abuse," *Journal of Marriage and the Family* 43 (1981): 675–92.

47. Hornung, McCullough, and Sugimoto, "Status Relationships in Marriage."

48. G. T. Hotaling and D. B. Sugarman, "An Analysis of Risk Markers in Husband-to-Wife Violence," *Journal of Family Violence* 5 (1990): 1–13; K. G. Kaufman, J. L. Jasinski, and E. Aldarondo, "Sociocultural Status and Incidence of Marital Violence in Hispanic Families," *Violence and Victims* 9 (3) (1994): 207–22.

49. Frieze and Browne, "Violence in Marriage," 163–218; D. Levinson, *Violence in Cross-Cultural Perspective*, Newbury Park, CA: Sage, 1989).

50. D. Sobsey, *Violence and Abuse in the Lives of People with Disabilities: The End of Silent Acceptance?* (Baltimore: Paul H. Brookes Publishing, 1994); D. Sobsey and C. Varnhagen, "Sexual Abuse, Assault, and Exploitation of Individuals with Disabilities," *Child Sexual Abuse: Critical Perspectives on Prevention, Intervention, and Treatment*, ed. C. Gagley and R. J. Thomlinson (Toronto: Wall and Emerson, 1991), 203–216.

51. M. P. Johnson, "Patriarchal Terrorism and Common Couple Violence: Two Forms of Violence Against Women," *Journal of Marriage and the Family* 57 (1995): 283–94.

52. U.S. Department of Justice, Bureau of Justice Statistics, "Criminal Victimization," 2003.

53. Tjaden and Thoennes, "Extent, Nature and Consequences of Intimate Partner Violence: Findings from the National Violence Against Women Survey."

54. Steven R. Tracy, "Clergy Responses to Domestic Violence," *Priscilla Papers* 21:2 (spring 2007): 9–16.

55. Cited by James Alsdurf and Phyllis Alsdurf, *Battered into Submission: The Tragedy of Wife Abuse in the Christian Home* (Eugene, OR: Wipf & Stock, 1998), 85.

Chapter 5: What Are the Effects of Domestic Violence?

1. Jennifer Erin Beste, *God and the Victim: Traumatic Intrusion on Grace and Freedom* (New York: Oxford University Press, 2007), 5.

2. R. Kotulak, *Inside the Brain: Revolutionary Discoveries of How the Mind Works* (Kansas City: Andrew McMeel Publishing, 1997); J. LeDoux, *The Emotional Brain: The Mysterious Underpinnings of Emotional Life* (New York: Touchstone, 1998); S. A. Raskin, "The Relationship between Sexual Abuse and Mild Traumatic Brain Injury," *Brain Injury* 11 (1997): 587–603; M. H. Scheutzow and D. R.Wiercisiewski, "Panic Disorder in a Patient with Traumatic Brain Injury: A Case Report and Discussion," *Brain Injury* 9 (1999): 705–14; B. A. Van der Kolk, A. C. McFarlane, and L. Weisaeth, eds, *Traumatic Stress: The Effects of Overwhelming Experience on Mind, Body, and Society* (New York: Guilford Press, 1996).

3. J. L. Herman, *Trauma and Recovery: The Aftermath of Violence—From Domestic Abuse to Political Terror* (New York: Basic Books, 1992); Raskin, "The Relationship between Sexual Abuse and Mild Traumatic Brain Injury"; Scheutzow and Wiercisiewski, "Panic Disorder in a Patient with Traumatic Brain Injury"; Van der Kolk, McFarlane, and Weisaeth, eds., *Traumatic Stress*.

4. J. LeDoux, *The Emotional Brain*; Y. I. Sheline, M. Sanghavi, M. A. Mintum et al., "Depression Duration but not Age Predicts Hippocampal Volume Loss in Medically Healthy Women with Recurrent Major Depression," *The Journal of Neuroscience* 19 (1999): 5034–43; Van der Kolk, McFarlane, and Weisaeth, eds, *Traumatic Stress*.

5. Susan Ress et al., "Lifetime Prevalence of Gender-Based Violence in Women and the Relationship with Mental Disorders and Psychosocial Function," *Journal of the American Medical Association* 306:5 (2011): 513–21.

6. S. E. Barkan and L. T. Gary, "Woman Abuse and Pediatrics: Expanding the Web of Detection," *Journal of the American Medical Women's Association* 51 (1996): 96–100; P. A. Barrier, "Domestic Violence," *Mayo Clinic Proc.* 73 (1998): 271–74; J. C. Campbell and K. L. Soeken, "Women's Responses to Battering: A Test of the Model," *Research in Nursing and Health* 22 (1999): 49–58.

7. K. N. Hartzell, A. A. Botek, and S. H. Goldberg, "Orbital Fractures in Women Due to Sexual Assault," *Ophthalmology* 103 (1996): 953–57.

8. D. Gaffigan-Bender and M. Narula, "Domestic Violence: Listening for the Truths That Patients Are Afraid to Tell," *Physical Therapy Magazine* (1998): 72–84; S. M. Hadley, "Working with Battered Women in the Emergency Department: A Model Program," *Journal of Emergency Nursing* 18 (1992): 18–23.

9. Barkan and Gary, "Woman Abuse and Pediatrics"; Gaffigan-Bender and Narula, "Domestic Violence: Listening for the Truths That Patients Are Afraid to Tell"; Muelleman, Reuwer, Sanson et al., "An Emergency Medicine Approach to Violence throughout the Life Cycle," *Academic Emergency Medicine* 3 (1996): 708–15; Van der Kolk, McFarlane, and Weisaeth, eds., *Traumatic Stress*.

10. Ann Jones and Susan Schecter, *When Loves Goes Wrong: When to Do When You Can't Do Anything Right. Strategies for Women with Controlling Partners* (New York: HarperCollins, 1992), 42–44.

11. Carol J. Adams, *Woman Battering* (Minneapolis: Fortress, 1994), 17–20.

12. Helen L. Conway, *Domestic Violence and the Church* (Carlisle, Cumbria: Paternoster Press, 1998), 26

13. C. Everett Koop, "From the Surgeon General, U.S. Public Health Service," *Journal of the American Medical Association* 267 (1992): 3132.

14. "Violence Against Women, A Majority Staff Report," Committee on the Judiciary, United States Senate, 102nd Congress, October 1992, 3; Gaffigan-Bender and Narula, "Domestic Violence: Listening for the Truths That Patients Are Afraid to Tell"; J. A. Grisso, A. R. Wishner, D. F. Schwarz et al., "A Population-Based Study of Injuries in Inner-City Women," *American Journal of Epidemiology* 134 (1991): 59–66; L. E. Keller, "Invisible Victims: Battered Women in Psychiatric and Medical Emergency Rooms," *Bulletin of the Menninger Clinic* 60 (1996): 1–21; A. C. Novello, "From the Surgeon General, U.S. Public Health Services: A Medical Response to Domestic Violence," *Journal of the American Medical Association* 267 (1992): 3132; S. Y. Melvin and M. C. Rhyne, "Domestic Violence," *Advanced Internal Medicine* 43 (1998): 1–25; and Patricia Tjaden and Nancy Thoennes, "Extent, Nature, and Consequences of intimate Partner Violence: Findings from the National Violence Against Women Survey"; (Washington, D.C.: U.S. Department of Justice, National Institute of Justice, 2000.)

15. U.S. Department of Justice, Bureau of Justice Statistics, "Intimate Partner Violence in the United States," December 2006.

16. Tjaden and Thoennes, "Stalking in America", National Institute for Justice, 1988.

17. M. C. Black, K. C. Basile, M. J. Breiding, S. G. Smith, M. L. Walters, M. T. Merrick, J. Chen, and M. R. Stevens, "The National Intimate Partner and Sexual Violence Survey: 2010 Summary Report" (Atlanta: National Center for Injury Prevention and Control, Centers for Disease Control and Prevention, 2011).

18. Tjaden and Thoennes, "Stalking in America".

19. James A. Mercy and Linda E. Saltzman, "Fatal Violence among Spouses in the United States, 1976–85," *American Journal of Public Health* 79 (1989): 595–99; James E. Bailey, Arthur L. Kellermann, Grant W. Somes, Joyce G. Banton, Frederick P. Rivara, and Norman B. Rushforth, "Risk Factors for Violent Death of Women in the Home," *Archives of Internal Medicine* 157 (7) (1997): 777–82; and Ronet Bachman and Linda E. Saltzman, "Violence Against Women: Estimates from the Redesigned Survey," Washington, DC: U.S. Department of Justice, Bureau of Justice Statistics and National Institute of Justice, 1995 (NCJ 154348).

20. Callie Marie Rennison and Sarah Welchans, "Intimate Partner Violence," U.S. Department of Justice: Bureau of Justice Statistics Special Report, May 2000, rev. January 31, 2002; Crime in the United States, 2000, Federal Bureau of Investigation: Uniform Crime Reports, 2001.

21. Office of Justice Programs, "Violence by Intimates: Analysis of Data on Crimes by Current or Former Spouses, Boyfriends, and Girlfriends," Bureau of Justice Statistics Factbook (Washington, DC: U.S. Department of Justice, March 1998), NCJ 167237.

22. Jacquelyn C. Campbell, "If I Can't Have You, No One Can: Power and Control in Homicide of Female Partners," in *Femicide: The Politics of Woman Killing*, ed. Jill Radford and Diana E. H. Russell (New York: Twayne Publishers, 1992), 99–113; and Linda Langford, Nancy Isaac, and Stacey Kabat, "Homicides Related to Intimate Partner Violence in Massachusetts," *Homicide Studies* 2(4) (1998): 353–77; and J. C. Campbell, D. Webster, J. Koziol-McLain, C. R. Block, D. Campbell, M. A. Curry, F. Gary, J. McFarlane, C. Sachs, P. Sharps, Y. Ulrich,

and S.A. Wilt, "Assessing Risk Factors for Intimate Partner Homicide," *National Institute of Justice Journal* 250 (November 2003): 14–19, NCJ 196547

23. Bureau of Justice Statistics, "Intimate Partner Violence in the U.S." 1993–2004, 2006.

24. George Pataki, "Intimate Partner Homicides in New York State" (Albany, NY: State of New York, 1997); Office of Justice Programs, Violence by Intimates; Campbell, "If I Can't Have You, No One Can;" Judith M. McFarlane, Jacquelyn C. Campbell, Susan A. Wilt, Carolyn J. Sachs, Yvonne Ulrich, and Xiao Xu, "Stalking and Intimate Partner Femicide," *Homicide Studies* 3:4 (1999) 300–316; Jacquelyn C. Campbell, *Assessing Dangerousness: Violence by Sexual Offenders, Batterers, and Child Abusers* (Newbury Park, CA: Sage, 1995); and J. C. Campbell, D. Webster, J. Koziol-McLain, C.R. Block, D. Campbell, M.A. Curry, F. Gary, J. McFarlane, C. Sachs, P. Sharps, Y. Ulrich, and S.A. Wilt, "Assessing Risk Factors for Intimate Partner Homicide," *National Institute of Justice Journal* 250 (November 2003): 14–19, NCJ 196547.

25. B. L. Stancliff, "Invisible Victims: Alert Practitioners Can Help Identify Domestic Abuse," *OT Practice* 2 (1997): 23.

26. J. C. Campbell and K. Soeken. "Forced Sex and Intimate Partner Violence: Effects on Women's Risk and Women's Health"; *Violence Against Women* 5:2 (July 1999): 1017–35; and Campbell, "Assessing Risk Factors for Intimate Partner Homicide"; R. Acierno, H. S. Resnick, and D. G. Kilpatrick, "Health Impact of Interpersonal Violence: Prevalence Rates, Case Identification, and Risk Factors for Sexual Assault, Physical Assault, and Domestic Violence in Men and Women," *Behavioral Medicine* 23 (1997): 53–64; J. P. Quillan, "Screening for Spousal or Partner Abuse in a Community Health Setting," *Journal of the American Academy of Nurse Practitioners* 8 (1996): 155–60.

27. M. C. Black, K. C. Basile, M. J. Breiding, S. G. Smith, M. L. Walters, M. T. Merrick, J. Chen, and M. R. Stevens, "The National Intimate Partner and Sexual Violence Survey: 2010 Summary Report," Atlanta, GA: National Center for Injury Prevention and Control, Centers for Disease Control and Prevention, 2011.

28. Catherine Clark Kroeger and Nancy Nason-Clark, *No Place for Abuse: Biblical and Practical Resources to Counteract Domestic Violence* (Downers Grove, IL: InterVarsity, 2001), 49–54.

29. Adams, *Woman Battering*, 17–19.

30. W. Proudfoot, "Religious Experience, Emotion, and Belief," *Harvard Theological Review* 70 no. 3/4 (1977): 348.

31. Matthew A. Elliott, *Faithful Feelings: Rethinking Emotion in the New Testament* (Grand Rapids: Kregel, 2006), 31.

32. Dan B. Allender and Tremper Longman III, *The Cry of the Soul: How Our Emotions Reveal Our Deepest Questions about God* (Colorado Springs: Navpress, 1994), 13

33. Paul Holmer, *Making Christian Sense* (Louisville: Westminster, 1984), 24.

34. Don E. Saliers, *Soul in Paraphrase: Prayer and Religious Affections* (Nitro, WV: OSL, 1991), 11.

35. Carl Trueman, *Fools Rush in Where Monkeys Fear to Tread* (Phillipsburg, NJ: P&R Publishing, 2012), 213.

Chapter 6: Does the Grace of God Apply to Me?

1. Adapted from *Rid of My Disgrace* by Justin S. Holcomb and Lindsey A. Holcomb, ©2011. Used by permission of Crossway, a publishing ministry of Good News Publishers, Wheaton, IL 60187, www.crossway.org.

2. The gospel is the announcement that Jesus (the God-man) lived a perfect life, died in our place, and rose from the dead. Those who trust in the person and work of Jesus receive the good news that God's "No" went to Jesus and God's "Yes" is all He will ever say to them. Your sins are forgiven and you are declared righteous. You are an adopted child of God.

3. John R. W. Stott, *Christ the Controversialist: A Study in Some Essentials of Evangelical Religion* (Downers Grove, IL: InterVarsity, 1970), 214.

4. Paul F. M. Zahl, *The Christianity Primer: Two Thousand Years of Amazing Grace* (Birmingham: Palladium Press, 2005), 7.

5. Paul F. M. Zahl, *Grace in Practice: A Theology of Everyday Life* (Grand Rapids: Eerdmans, 2007), 64.

Chapter 7: What Does the Bible Say about Women?

1. R. G. Branch, "Eve," in *Dictionary of the Old Testament: Pentateuch*, ed. T. Desmond Alexander and David W. Baker (Downers Grove, IL.: InterVarsity, 2003), 240.

2. Wayne Grudem, *Systematic Theology: An Introduction to Biblical Doctrine* (Grand Rapids: Zondervan, 1994), 455.

3. James B. Hurley, *Man and Woman in Biblical Perspective* (Grand Rapids: Zondervan, 1981), 21.

4. Ibid., 22.

5. Ibid., 29–30.

6. William J. Webb, *Slaves, Women, and Homosexuals: Exploring the Hermeneutics of Cultural Analysis* (Downers Grove, IL: InterVarsity, 2001), 76.

7. Tikva Frymer-Kensky, "Sex and Sexuality," in *The Anchor Bible Dictionary*, ed. David Noel Freedman, vol. 5 (New York: Doubleday, 1992), 1145.

8. Craig L. Blomberg, "Woman," in *Baker Theological Dictionary of the Bible*, ed. Walter A. Elwell (Grand Rapids: Baker, 1996), 825.

9. Ben Witherington, III, *Women in the Ministry of Jesus: A Study of Jesus' Attitudes to Women and Their Roles as Reflected in His Earthly Life*, Society for New Testament Studies Monograph Series 51 (Cambridge: Cambridge University Press, 1984), 120.

10. Ibid., 125–26.

11. Blomberg, "Woman," 826.

12. Grant R. Osborne, "Women in Jesus' Ministry," *Westminster Theological Journal* 51:2 (Fall 1989): 274.

13. Blomberg, "Woman," 826.

14. Nicole, "Woman, Biblical Concept of," *Evangelical Dictionary of Theology*, ed. Walter A. Elwell (Grand Rapids: Baker), 2001.

15. Hurley, *Man and Woman in Biblical Perspective*, 116.

16. Ibid., 117.

17. Ibid., 124.

18. Pliny, *Letter* 10.96–97, http://www.fordham.edu/halsall/source/pliny1.asp.

19. Witherington, *Women in the Ministry of Jesus*, 127.

20. Alvin J. Schmidt, *How Christianity Changed the World* (Grand Rapids: Zondervan, 2004), 102–3.

21. Nicole, "Woman, Biblical Concept of," 1285.

Chapter 8: What Does the Bible Say about Violence against Women?

1. Quoted in Susan Hall, "The Theology of Domestic Violence," *Views from the Edge* (Seattle: Mars Hill Graduate School, January 2006), 1–2.

2. This message can be particularly empowering for abuse victims. In one study of abused Christian women, when asked what they most needed from the church, abused women indicated two primary needs: (1) the church's recognition that violence against women and children is a problem even in the church and (2) a straightforward condemnation of domestic violence from the pulpit. See Nancy Nason-Clark, "Conservative Protestants and Violence against Women: Exploring the Rhetoric and the Response," in *Sex, Lies, and Sanctity: Deviance and Religion in Contemporary America*, edited by Mary Jo Neitz and Marion S. Goldman (Greenwich, CT: JAI Press, 1995), 123–24.

3. For a survey of some of the biblical data on physical abuse, see Catherine Clark Kroeger and Nancy Nason-Clark, *No Place for Abuse: Biblical and Practical Resources to Counteract Domestic Violence* (Downers Grove, IL.: InterVarsity, 2001), and Steven Tracy, *Mending the Soul: Understanding and Healing Abuse* (Grand Rapids: Zondervan, 2005).

4. Ron Clark, *Setting the Captives Free: A Christian Theology for Domestic Violence* (Eugene, OR: Cascade, 2005), 138.

5. J. David Pleins, "Poor, Poverty," in *The Anchor Bible Dictionary*, ed. David Noel Freedman, vol. 5 (New York: Doubleday, 1992), 408.

6. Ibid., 409.

7. Ulrike Bail, "'O God, Hear My Prayer': Psalm 55 and Violence Against Women," in *A Feminist Companion Wisdom and Psalms*, ed. Athalya Brenner and Carole R. Fontaine (Sheffield, England: Shef¬field Academic Press, 1998), 249.

8. Ibid., 138.

9. Cornelius Plantinga, *Not the Way It's Supposed to Be* (Grand Rapids: Eerdmans, 1995), 30.

Chapter 9: What Does the Bible Say about God Delivering Victims?

1. Carol J. Adams, *Woman Battering* (Philadelphia: Fortress, 1994), 105.

2. R. E. O. White, "Violence," in *Evangelical Dictionary of Theology*, ed. Walter A. Elwell, 2nd ed. (Grand Rapids: Baker, 2001), 1246–47.

3. Scot McKnight, "Salvation and Deliverance Imagery," in *Dictionary of the Old Testament: Wisdom, Poetry & Writings*, ed. Tremper Longman III and Peter Enns (Downers Grove, IL: InterVarsity, 2008), 710–14. McKnight writes: "By far the greatest concentration of salvation and deliverance imagery in our literature is found in the psalms, which are the focus of this article. As the ordinary Israelite appealed to the king for deliverance [2 Sam 14:4], so too the psalmist, who by tradition frequently was King David, appealed to God for deliverance [Ps 12:1] from his personal, tribal and national enemies.... Images of salvation and deliverance abound in the book of Psalms, with the root for 'save' [yasha'] appearing in almost half the psalms. And God, who is present in the temple, is therefore praised and exalted for his salvation. Indeed, the act of praise is a multifaceted act of faith, protest and hope ... The God of Israel is the God of salvation ... However, even if the focus in the psalms is on the psalmists' more physical dangers and national condition, one psalm stands tall as a focus on personal forgiveness and redemption from sin: Psalm 51. David has committed murder, and he pleads with the 'God of my salvation' for forgiveness from 'bloodshed' (Psalm 51:14).... A central notion of salvation is seen in Psalm 31:1: 'In your righteousness deliver me.' God's righteousness is God's saving faithfulness that results in deliverance, surely evoking God's covenant faithfulness from the days of Abraham. Notice how each of these terms fills the others with meaning: 'Your steadfast love, O LORD, extends to the heavens, your faithfulness to the clouds. Your righteousness is like the mighty mountains, your judgments are like the great deep; you save humans and animals alike, O LORD' (Ps 36:6 NRSV). God's steadfast love, faithfulness, righteousness and judgments lead to the psalmist's salvation." Another scholar writes that "within the OT, at least one of the basic identifications of God is as the one who saved Israel: 'Yahweh your God, who brought you up out of Egypt, out of the land of slavery.' While the 'God of Abraham, Isaac, and Jacob' formula and the covenant formula ('I will be your God, and you will be my people') are less straightforwardly about salvation than about election, the covenant, at least, should probably be seen in soteriological terms. For Israel to be God's people means that God has saved and will save Israel. In the NT, the message of salvation is even more central. 'You are to name him Jesus, for he will save his people ...' (Matt. 1:21 NRSV) is the fundamental announcement, and the Pauline corpus regularly describes Christians as those who are being saved." Stephen R. Holmes, "Salvation, Doctrine of," in *Dictionary for Theological Interpretation of the Bible*, ed. Kevin J. Vanhoozer (Grand Rapids: Baker, 2005), 711.

4. Colin Brown, *The New International Dictionary of New Testament Theology*, ed. Colin Brown (Grand Rapids: Zondevan, 1978), 3:205.

5. Leon Morris, "Salvation," in *Dictionary of Paul and His Letters*, ed. Gerald F. Hawthorne and Ralph P. Martin (Downers Grove, IL: InterVarsity, 1993), 858. This latter idea is more prevalent in Paul, where "the important thing is deliverance from sin and from the consequences of sin, though it is much more common for Paul to speak simply of salvation than to say what people are saved from.

... For Paul 'salvation' refers to what Christ has done in his great saving act for sinners; all the Pauline passages bear on this act in some way. It is central to the Pauline understanding of Christianity, for salvation is the very purpose of the incarnation of the Son of God: 'Christ Jesus came into the world to save sinners' (1 Tim 1:15). Salvation is a comprehensive word bringing out the truth that God in Christ has rescued people from the desperate state that their sins had brought about."

6. Walter Brueggemann, *Old Testament Theology: Essays on Structure, Theme, and Text* (Minneapolis: Fortress, 1992), 29.

Chapter 10: Does the Bible Say I Should Suffer Abuse and Violence?

1. Patrici Tjaden a and Nancy Thoennes, "Extent, Nature and Consequences of Intimate Partner Violence: Findings from the National Violence Against Women Survey" (2000). National Institute of Justice and the Centers for Disease Control and Prevention.

2. Susan Hall, "The Theology of Domestic Violence," *Views from the Edge* (Seattle: Mars Hill Graduate School, January 2006), 1.

3. R. T. France, *The Gospel of Matthew, New International Commentary on the New Testament* (Grand Rapids: Eerdmans, 2007), 466 n. 1.

4. Ibid., 469.

5. D. A. Carson, *The Gospel according to John, Pillar New Testament Commentary* (Grand Rapids: Eerdmans, 1991), 358.

6. John B. Polhill, *Acts, New American Commentary*, vol. 26 (Nashville: Broadman, 1992), 464.

7. Darrell Bock, *Acts, Baker Exegetical Commentary on the New Testament* (Grand Rapids: Baker, 2007), 665.

8. Craig Keener cogently argues that physical abuse is conceptually a form of infidelity that breaks the marriage contract Craig Keener, *And Marries Another: Divorce and Remarriage in the Teachings of the New Testament* (Peabody, MA.: Hendrickson, 1991), 105–9. In a more recent detailed study of divorce and remarriage, David Instone-Brewer argues based on 1 Corinthians 7 and Exod. 21:10–11 that emotional and material abuse (neglect) are grounds for divorce (*Divorce and Remarriage in the Bible: The Social and Literary Context* [Grand Rapids: Eerdmans, 2002]), 275. David Clyde Jones lands in a similar place to Instone-Brewer but on slightly different grounds. After surveying the biblical evidence, he asks the question of whether Jesus' exception clause states the one and only exception. "If so, does porneia have an exclusively sexual reference?" (See David Clyde Jones, *Biblical Christian Ethics* [Grand Rapids: Baker, 1994], 202. The entire chapter "Divorce and Remarriage" is quite helpful, p 177–204). His answer is that, based on Paul's allowance for divorce on the grounds of abandonment in 1 Corinthians 7:15, we must conclude that either porneia "is not the one and only ground for divorce, or it does not have an exclusively sexual reference in the exceptive clause" (202). He continues, "The only satisfying approach to this question is by way of the analogy of faith, which seeks the theological rationale that unites the two exceptive passages. Why is adultery (which is at least included in the term porneia) cause sufficient for dissolving the bond

of marriage? Because it is a radical breach of marital fidelity, violating the commitment of exclusive conjugal love. Why does the departure of the unbeliever in a mixed marriage leave the believer free to remarry? Because it is a radical breach of marital fidelity, violating the commitment of lifelong companionship. The exceptional circumstance common to both instances is willful and radical violation of the marriage covenant" (202). He later concludes that "the adulterer, the deserter, and the inveterate abuser are alike guilty of gross betrayal of their marriage companion. By their actions they willfully repudiate the one-flesh relationship of the marriage covenant and so provide just cause for the dissolution of the marriage bond" (204).

9. Ron Clark, *Setting the Captives Free: A Christian Theology of Domestic Violence* (Eugene, OR: Wipf & Stock, 2005), 172.

10. Erin Dufault-Hunter, "Spousal Abuse," in *Dictionary of Scripture and Ethics*, ed. Joel B. Green (Grand Rapids: Baker, 2011), 747.

11. Marie F. Fortune, "The Transformation of Suffering: A Biblical and Theological Perspective," in *Christianity, Patriarchy, and Abuse: A Feminist Critique*, ed. Joanne Carlson Brown and Carole R. Brown (Cleveland: Pilgrim, 1989), 145.

12. Ibid., 144–45.

13. Johanna W. H. van Wijk-Bos, "Violence and the Bible," in *Telling the Truth: Preaching about Sexual and Domestic Violence* , ed. John S. McClure and Nancy J. Ramsay (Cleveland: United Church, 1998), 32–33. On page 32, Wijk-Bos writes: "The liberative word from the Bible issues from the biblical indictment of relationships of violence as contrary to God's intent for the creation and the community called into covenant with God. Law and prophets denounce such relationships as destructive of the community's relationship to God."

Chapter 11: You Save Me from Violence: Psalm 18

1. Psalm 18. This is identical to 2 Samuel 22:2–20. For more on this song, see P. Kyle McCarter, Jr., *II Samuel*, Anchor Bible, vol. 9 (Garden City, NY: Doubleday, 1984), 473; Derek Kidner, *Psalms 1–72*, *Tyndale Old Testament Commentaries* (Downers Grove, IL: InterVarsity, 1973), 91. Frank Moore Cross, Jr. and David Noel Freedman, "A Royal Song of Thanksgiving: II Samuel 22 = Psalm 18," *Journal of Biblical Literature* 72 [1953]: 15–34; A. A. Anderson, *2 Samuel*, Word Biblical Commentary, vol. 11 (Nashville: Thomas Nelson, 1989), 262; Gnana Robinson, *Let Us Be like the Nations: A Commentary on the Books of 1 and 2 Samuel*, International Theological Commentary (Grand Rapids: Eerdmans, 1993).

2. As in the NIV [cf. 22:49, 'ish hamas]. So also McCarter Jr., *II Samuel* (1984), 455.

3. Genesis 6:11, 13; 16:5; 49:5; Exodus 23:1; Deuteronomy 19:16; Judges 9:24; 2 Samuel 22:3, 49; 1 Chronicles 12:18; Job 16:17; 19:7; Psalms 7:17; 11:5; 18:49; 25:19; 27:12; 35:11; 55:10; 58:3; 72:14; 73:6, 13–14; 74:20; 140:2, 5, 12; Proverbs 3:31; 4:17; 8:36; 10:6, 11; 13:2; 16:29; 26:6; Isaiah 53:9; 59:6; 60:18; Jeremiah 6:7; 13:22; 20:8; 22:3; 51:35, 46; Lamentations 2:6; Ezekiel 7:11, 23; 8:17; 12:19; 22:26; 28:16; 45:9; Joel 4:19; Amos 3:10; 6:3; Obadiah 1:10; Jonah 3:8; Micah 6:12; Habakkuk 1:2f, 9; 2:8, 17; Zephaniah 1:9; 3:4; Malachi 2:16.

4. The different shades of meaning of the noun form "can be seen from the variety of its synonyms," which include words like "iniquity," "pride," "blood," "evil way," "ruin," "sickness," "contention," "insensitivity," "wounds," "wickedness," "oppression," "lies," and "destruction." See H. Haag, "chāmās," in *Theological Dictionary of the Old Testament*, ed. G. J. Botterweck and H. Ringgren, trans. D. E. Green, vol. 4 (Grand Rapids: Eerdmans, 1994), 480.

5. Francis Brown, S. R. Driver, and Charles A Briggs, *Brown-Driver-Briggs Hebrew and English Lexicon* (Peabody, MA: Hendrickson, 2001), 329; L. Koehler, W. Baumgartner, and J. J. Stamm, *The Hebrew and Aramaic Lexicon of the Old Testament*, trans. and ed. M. E. J. Richardson, vol. 1 (Leiden: Brill, 1994), 329.

6. The most common synonym, from shadad, has to do primarily with the oppression of the poor and "even suggests this is the basic meaning" of the word. Haag, "chāmās," 480.

7. Exodus 23:1; Deuteronomy 19:16; Job 16:17; 19:17; 21:27; Psalms 27:12; 35:11.

8. Haag, "chāmās," 486.

9. Ibid., 481.

10. There is no parallel in Psalm 18 to its use in 2 Samuel 22:3. In the LXX it is translated with varied words, most often *adikia*, "wrongdoing, injustice." See ibid.

11. Anderson, *2 Samuel*, Word Biblical Commentary, 263.

12. Eugene H. Peterson, *First and Second Samuel*, Westminster Bible Companion (Louisville: Westminster John Knox, 1999), 248.

13. Joyce G. Baldwin, *1 and 2 Samuel*, Tyndale Old Testament Commentaries (Downers Grove, IL:InterVarsity, 1988), 287. On David's use of metaphor and his awareness of the presence of God, Peterson writes, "The single most characteristic thing about David is his relationship to God.... The largest part of David's existence is not David, it is God. The evidence for David's pervasive, saturated awareness of God is in his profusion of metaphor: rock, fortress, deliverer, refuge, shield, horn of salvation, stronghold, savior. David is immersed in God. Every visibility reveals an invisibility. David names God by metaphor. Metaphor is the witness of language that there is a comprehensive interconnectedness to life invisible and visible, that is, 'heaven and earth.' Everything seen and heard, tasted, touched, and experienced, if only followed far enough and deeply enough, brings us into the presence of God." See Peterson, *Samuel*, 248–49.

14. Robinson, *Let Us Be Like the Nations*, 271–72.

15. As a young boy, David would kill a lion or bear to protect his sheep, and when it comes time to battle Goliath. he says, "The LORD who delivered me from the paw of the lion and from the paw of the bear will deliver me from the hand of this Philistine" (1 Sam. 17:37). Though David lives on the run from Saul, he is saved from him again and again until finally Saul is killed and David is made king. David is a victorious warrior throughout his life because the hand of God is with him (e.g., see 2 Sam. 8). David is not perfect, as his sin with Bathsheba shows, and for which God disciplines him. But as he humbled himself before the Lord and trusted in him, God was faithful to deliver him from his enemies, and this is the theme of 2 Samuel 22 and Psalm 18.

Chapter 12: Will God Remain Faithful?: Psalm 22

1. Psalm 22 is famous for the quotations found in the account in John 19 of Jesus' crucifixion. But maybe, with a better understanding of the whole psalm, its use in the narrative of Jesus' crucifixion will become richer and more striking.

2. By way of background, it is important to remember that David's exile from Saul came after he had accrued a wife, house, and a great deal of wealth as a warrior in Saul's army.

3. Marie F. Fortune, "The Transformation of Suffering: A Biblical and Theological Perspective," in *Christianity, Patriarchy, and Abuse: A Feminist Critique*, ed. Joanne Carlson Brown and Carole R. Brown (Cleveland: Pilgrim, 1989), 139.

4. Carol J. Adams, *Woman Battering* (Philadelphia, Fortress, 1994), 107.

5. Ibid., 108.

Chapter 13: But I Will Trust in You: Psalm 55

1. Derek Kidner, "Such a cry as this helps to make the Psalter a book for the extremities of experience as well as for it normalities." Derek Kidner, *Psalms 1–72*, Tyndale Old Testament Commentaries (Downers Grove, IL: InterVarsity, 1973), 199.

2. Robert G. Bratcher and William D. Reyburn, *A Translator's Handbook on the Book of Psalms* (New York: United Bible Societies, 1991), 491.

3. Kidner, *Psalms 1–72*, 199–202. The ESV Study Bible breaks it up in the same way as Kidner. For more on the structure and outline of the Psalms, also see John Goldingay, *Psalms*, vol. 2 (Grand Rapids: Baker, 2007), 165–66; and Marin E. Tate, *Psalms 51–100*, Word Biblical Commentary, vol. 20 (Dallas: Word, 1990), 56.

4. Kidner, *Psalms 1–72*, 199. The same connection is mentioned by A. A. Anderson, *The Book of Psalms*, vol. 1 (Grand Rapids: Eerdmans, 1972), 412.

5. Ibid., 168.

6. F. Delitzsch, *Psalms*, trans. Francis Bolton, *Commentary on the Old Testament*, vol. 5 (Peabody, MA: Hendrickson, 2001), 383.

7. Ulrike Bail, "'O God, Hear My Prayer': Psalm 55 and Violence Against Women," in *A Feminist Companion Wisdom and Psalms*, ed. Athalya Brenner and Carole R. Fontaine (Sheffield, England: Sheffield Academic Press, 1998), 249.

8. Ibid., 250.

9. Ibid., 251.

10. Ulrike Bail, "The Breath after the Comma, Psalm 55 and Violence Against Women," *Journal of Religion and Abuse* 1:3, 13; and Gerald T. Sheppard, "'Enemies and the Politics of Prayer in the Book of the Psalms," in David Jobling, Peggy L. Day, and Gerald T. Sheppard eds. *The Bible and the Politics of Exegesis: Essays in Honor of Norman K. Gottwald on His Sixty-Fifth Birthday* (Cleveland: Pilgrims Press, 1991), 77.

11. Ibid.

12. Taken from the ESV Study Bible.

13. Anderson, *Psalms*, 416.

14. Bail, "'O God, Hear My Prayer': Psalm 55 and Violence Against Women," 251.

15. Kidner, *Psalms 1–72*, 201.

16. Ibid., 202.

17. Hossfeld, *Psalms*, 56, quoting Ulrike Bail, *Gegen das Schweigen klagen* (Gütersloh: Chr. Kaiser/Gütersloher Verlagshaus, 1998), 175.

18. Kidner, *Psalms 1–72*, 202.

19. Goldingay, *Psalms*, 179.

20. Quoting Bail, "'O God, Hear My Prayer': Psalm 55 and Violence Against Women," 243.

21. Bail, Ibid., 257.

A Final Note

1. *Book of Common Prayer* (New York: Church Publishing, 1979), 389.

Appendix 2

1. We are thankful for Natalie Collins's work in developing a safety plan. We incorporated many of her suggestions and considerations.

Appendix 3

1. *Book of Common Prayer* (New York: Church Publishing, 1979), 260.

Recommended Reading and Bibliography

1. This reading list modifies Steven Tracy's list: http://www.mendingthesoul.org/recommended-reading/.

2. http://justinholcomb.com/bibliography-is-it-my-fault/.

Who are you, really?

MADE *for* MORE

An Invitation to Live in God's Image

HANNAH ANDERSON

978-0-8024-1032-0

Is your identity based on a role? By a relationship? Through your achievements? What does your family say about you? Who are you as a woman?

Honestly, these are not the right questions. The real question is, who are you as a woman created in God's image? When we grasp our identity in His we'll realize that we were made for so much more. Don't settle for seconds. Start your journey now to discover your true identity.

Also available as an ebook

MOODY
PUBLISHERS

WHERE DO I GO FROM HERE?

978-0-8024-0449-7

Life has a way of tilting. Jobs are lost. Children leave. Homes foreclose. Spouses die. Everyone experiences the loss of something or someone precious at some point. And more often than not a loss is unexpected, certainly unwanted, and can be our undoing.

Also available as an ebook

MOODY
PUBLISHERS

Brewing rich conversations, delivering bold truth.

Pour yourself a cup of coffee and enjoy **Java with Juli**, a new podcast by host and clinical psychologist Dr. Juli Slattery. From the cozy setting of a coffee shop, Juli offers a woman's perspective on intimacy and converses with guests about the challenges of being a contemporary Christian woman.

www.moodyradio.org/javawithjuli

MOODYRADIO
Where you turn. For life.